TOP 10 COSTA BLANCA

EYEWITNESS TRAVEL

Left **The "Enchanted City", Playa de Bolnuevo** Right **A delicious plate of local seafood**

LONDON, NEW YORK,
MELBOURNE, MUNICH AND DELHI
www.dk.com

Produced by DP Services,
31 Ceylon Road, London W14 OPY

Reproduced by Colourscan, Singapore
Printed and bound in China by
Leo Paper Products Ltd

First published in Great Britain in 2005
by Dorling Kindersley Limited
80 Strand, London WC2R 0RL
A Penguin Company

Reprinted with revisions 2007, 2009

A CIP catalogue record is available from the British Library.

ISBN: 978-1-4053-3979-7

Within each Top 10 list in this book, no hierarchy of quality or popularity is implied. All 10 are, in the editor's opinion, of roughly equal merit.

Contents

Costa Blanca's Top 10

The information in this DK Eyewitness Top 10 Travel Guide is checked regularly.

Every effort has been made to ensure that this book is as up-to-date as possible at the time of going to press. Some details, however, such as telephone numbers, opening hours, prices, gallery hanging arrangements and travel information are liable to change. The publishers cannot accept responsibility for any consequences arising from the use of this book, nor for any material on third party websites, and cannot guarantee that any website address in this book will be a suitable source of travel information. We value the views and suggestions of our readers very highly. Please write to: Publisher, DK Eyewitness Travel Guides, Dorling Kindersley, 80 Strand, London, WC2R 0RL Great Britain.

COVER: Front – **DK Images**: Tony Souter bl; **SuperStock**: Prisma main. Back: **DK Images** Tony Souter tc, tl, tr. Spine: **DK Images** John Miller b.

Left **Galería Dorada, Palau Ducal, Gandia (ceiling detail)** Right **Isla Tabarca**

Left **Catedral de Santa María, Murcia (Puerta del Perdón)** Right **Penyal d'Ifac, Calp**

COSTA BLANCA'S TOP10

COSTA BLANCA'S TOP 10

TOP 10 Costa Blanca Highlights

Sun, sea and sand are excellent reasons to visit the Costa Blanca, but its attractions don't stop there. Inland, you can explore magnificent Natural Parks, wild sierras and remote hill villages, or visit historic towns with fascinating museums and a wealth of fabulous architecture. The engaging capital cities of Alicante (Alacant) and Murcia are crammed with great shops and tapas bars, and a string of lively resorts along the coast offers splendid beaches, fantastic nightlife and plenty of opportunities for fun. Best of all, there's always a secret cove or rugged cape to be discovered if the crowds get too much.

1 Calblanque

Calblanque is a gorgeous stretch of unspoilt coastline, and one of the area's best-kept secrets. The golden beaches and quiet coves are peaceful even in the height of the tourist season *(see pp8–9)*.

2 Castillo de Santa Bárbara, Alicante

Visible for miles around, Alicante's dramatic castle looms high on a dusty pinnacle. Its sturdy ramparts and watchtowers offer spectacular views over the endless blue of the Mediterranean *(see pp10–13)*.

3 Guadalest

The enchanting hilltop village of Guadalest sits under the romantic ruins of a battered castle, and overlooks a beautiful valley with a deep turquoise lake *(see pp14–15)*.

4 Penyal d'Ifac (Peñón de Ifach)

A designated Natural Park, this extraordinary rock erupts spectacularly from the sea. The views from the summit are breathtaking *(see pp16–17)*.

Preceding pages **The hilltop village of Guadalest, with castle ruins and bell tower above**

5 Casa-Museo Modernista, Novelda

Every detail of this Art Nouveau-style town house is exquisite, from the sinuous staircase with its vine-leaf motif to the rainbow-coloured skylights *(see pp18–19)*.

6 Sierra de Espuña

A beautiful stretch of forest and craggy peaks, the Natural Park of Sierra de Espuña offers excellent hiking, a wealth of wildlife, and complete peace *(see pp20–21)*.

7 Hort del Cura, Elx (Elche)

This luxuriant garden, the most beautiful corner of the famous palm groves of Elx, is a tranquil enclave of tropical flowers and cactuses shaded by palm trees *(see pp22–3)*.

8 Isla Tabarca

The tiny island of Tabarca is rimmed with rocky coves and sandy beaches, and the surrounding marine reserve is a paradise for snorkellers and divers *(see pp24–5)*.

9 Palau Ducal, Gandia

This sumptuous Gothic palace, magnificently embellished over the centuries, was home to St Francis of Borja *(see pp26–7)*.

10 Catedral de Santa María, Murcia

Several centuries in the making, Murcia Cathedral is one of the finest Baroque buildings in Spain, with a frilly bell tower, a sumptuous façade and lavishly decorated chapels *(see pp28–31)*.

TOP 10 Calblanque

Calblanque, a gorgeous natural paradise near the Mar Menor, is one of the few stretches of Mediterranean coastline to have survived unspoilt – and virtually undiscovered. Thirteen kilometres of quiet coves, sandy beaches and rare fossilized dunes are set against a backdrop of pine forest and craggy hills, criss-crossed with excellent walking trails that offer beautiful panoramas at every turn. Salt lagoons attract a wealth of bird life, while the cliffs and hills are home to several unusual species of flora and fauna.

Local flora

The only café in the park is a small beach bar with erratic opening hours, so bring plenty of water and picnic supplies, which you can easily find in the nearby resort of La Manga.

Calblanque is poorly signposted. Take the Cartagena–La Manga motorway, leaving at the Calblanque exit about 1 km (half a mile) after Los Belones; the dirt road leads to the visitor information centre. The beaches have no wheelchair access.

- *Map P5*
- *Visitor information centre (La Jordana): 968 29 84 23*
- *Information point at Playa Negrete*
- *Free*

Top 10 Features

1. Beaches
2. Dunes
3. Coves
4. Walks and Rides
5. Flora and Fauna
6. Bird Life
7. Salinas del Rassall
8. Old Mines
9. Cliffs
10. Mountain Peaks

1 Beaches

Calblanque's beaches are the most beautiful in Murcia. Long stretches of golden sand are interspersed with small coves, overlooked by rippling dunes and cliffs. Most popular – yet still uncrowded – are Playa de las Cañas, Playa Calblanque, and Playa Larga *(main image)*.

2 Dunes

Wooden walkways traverse Calblanque's fragile dune system *(above)*, fossilized over millennia and sculpted by wind and sea into spell-binding shapes. The best back onto Cañas, Larga and Negrete Beaches.

3 Coves

The entire 13 km (8 mile) length of Calblanque's coastline is pocked with dozens of tiny coves, where the turquoise waters are perfect for diving and snorkelling. Even in the height of summer you can pick your way across the rocks to find one all to yourself *(below)*.

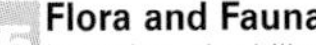

4 Walks and Rides
The Calblanque Natural Park is covered by a network of walking and mountain-biking trails *(above)* outlined in leaflets available at the park information office.

5 Flora and Fauna
In spring, the hills of Calblanque are carpeted with wild flowers. Among the pine forests are rarer trees, including one of the last surviving cypress groves in Spain. Foxes and badgers are common; you may even spot the endangered *tortuga mora* (sea turtle).

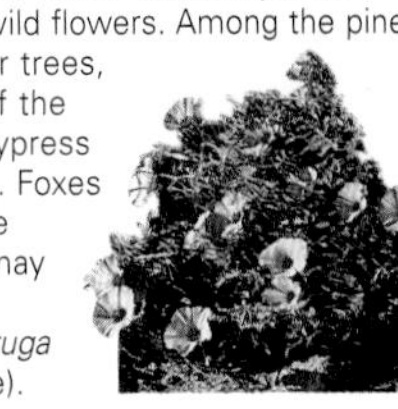

6 Bird Life
Calblanque is particularly rich in bird life. Among the species you may encounter are Bonelli's eagle, the eagle owl, Audoin's gull and the green woodpecker, as well as flamingoes and several varieties of heron and plover.

7 Salinas del Rasall
Still used for commercial salt production, the salt lakes of Rasall are a major nesting area for aquatic resident and migratory birds. The waters contain the brilliantly striped Fartet, an unusual and endangered fish.

8 Old Mines
On the outer fringes of the park you will see the ghostly remnants of abandoned tin, silver and copper mines *(above)*.

9 Cliffs
Calblanque's rugged yet ethereal cliffs offer spectacular views along the whole coastline.

10 Mountain Peaks
The mountains of Calblanque rarely rise above 300 m (984 ft), yet they offer breathtaking views across woods and out to sea *(below)*.

Genesis of a Regional Park

The tourist boom of the 1960s and 1970s transformed the once-tranquil region of the Mar Menor into a holiday mecca crammed with high-rise hotels and apartment buildings. In the early 1980s, yet more development was proposed south of La Manga, but the plans appalled local residents. After a protracted battle, the locals triumphed, and the area was finally declared a Regional Park in 1987, becoming one of the last unspoilt enclaves on the whole Mediterranean coast.

A section of the GR92, a long-distance walking path, snakes along the entire length of the Calblanque coastline.

TOP 10 Castillo de Santa Bárbara, Alicante

Visible for miles around, Alicante's castle looms dramatically above the city. The hill it commands has been inhabited since the Bronze Age, but it was not until the end of the 9th century that the Arabs built the first fortress here. Rebuilt during the 16th and 17th centuries, it was expanded into a mighty garrison during the 18th. You can climb up through a breezy pine forest, pausing in the stunning modern Parque de la Ereta on the way, or take the lazy option and be cranked up 200 m (656 ft) in a lift bored through the rock.

Castle picnic area

Within the castle complex, the Kiosko offers an expensive and limited menu of hot dogs, burgers and refreshments.

Let the lift take the strain out of getting up to the castle, but stroll back down to enjoy the two lovely parks along the way.

The castle complex has no information office, but maps are available within the galleries.

There is wheelchair access to the lift and central square only.

- *Mount Benacantil*
- *Map E5*
- *965 26 31 31*
- *Castle: Open Apr–Oct: 10am–8pm daily; Nov–Mar: 9am–7pm daily; Closed 1 Jan, 25 Dec. Free (return lift ticket: €2.40)*

Top 10 Features

1. Castle Complex
2. Parque de Ingenieros
3. Plaza del Cuartel
4. La Torreta
5. Cuartel de Ingenieros
6. Antiguo Cuerpo de Guardia
7. Ramparts and Terraces
8. Lift
9. Parks
10. Macho del Castillo

1 Castle Complex

Perched high on the lofty peak of Mount Benacantil, Alicante's castle is straight out of a story book. It's one of the largest surviving castles in Spain, an impressive complex of sturdy stone halls and spacious squares built over 900 years.

2 Parque de Ingenieros

Shaded with palms and scattered with wooden benches, the Parque de Ingenieros (Engineers' Park) is the prettiest and greenest of the castle's squares. The original Arab fortress, long demolished, once stood on this site.

3 Plaza del Cuartel

This wide, sun-bleached expanse at the centre of the fortress is dominated by the massive former barracks building *(cuartel)*, which contains a small exhibition on the development of the castle. Nearby, the snack kiosk and picnic area offer fine views.

4 La Torreta

This battered yet still graceful watchtower *(left)* is poised loftily over the main entrance into the castle. The oldest surviving structure in the whole complex, its base incorporates stones from the original Arab fortress.

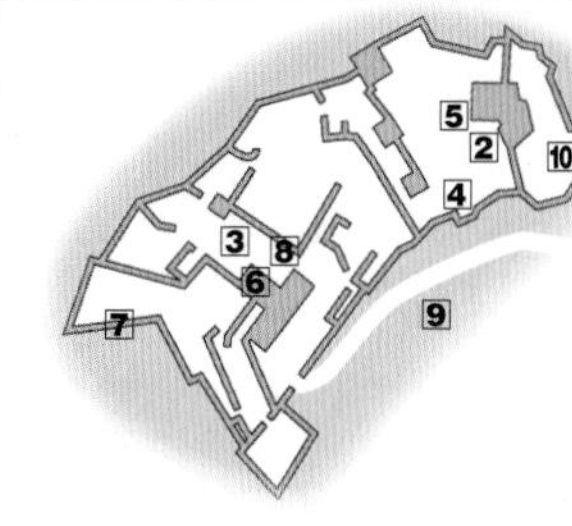

5 Cuartel de Ingenieros

One of the largest of the castle buildings, the Engineers' Barracks was erected in the 1700s, when the fortress was expanded. Now it makes a magnificent gallery for art exhibitions, as well as offering splendid views.

6 Antiguo Cuerpo de Guardia

In the 18th century, the castle tavern and the guardroom used to share this building – guard duty must have been popular! Now it contains galleries.

7 Ramparts and Terraces

You can stroll along vast sections of the massive fortifications which still encircle the castle. The views are spectacular.

8 Lift

This is no ordinary lift. If you can't face the long, hot climb to the top of the hill, it will swoop you up in seconds in to the heart of the castle. Tunnelled right through the rock, the lift starts from a cave-like entrance opposite the Postiguet Beach below.

9 Parks

The road up to the castle winds its way through the pine-shaded Parque Monte Benacantil. On the southern flank, the award-winning Parque de la Ereta includes a restaurant serving Mediterranean cuisine, an open-air cafeteria and an exhibition hall.

10 Macho del Castillo

The highest point of the whole complex is the Macho del Castillo, a wide, scrubby square, which offers the most spectacular views of all *(right)*. It is still scattered with rusting cannons, which poke threateningly through the fortifications in all directions.

Castle Views

Until recently, the vast halls and squares of the Castillo de Santa Bárbara provided a striking setting for the Capa family's extensive collection of 20th-century Spanish sculpture. The Capa collection has now moved to Madrid, but thanks to its strategic location on Mount Benacantil, the castle is still worth a visit. From here you can enjoy spectacular views over the city of Alicante (especially the roof terraces in the Old Town) and its surroundings.

Left **La Explanada** Centre **Basílica de Santa María** Right **Alicante's port**

Other Sights in Alicante (Alacant)

1 The Old Town (El Barrio)
Built around the slopes of Mount Benacantil, this area is attractive at any time of day or night. *Map U2*

2 La Explanada
Alicante's famous, palm-lined boulevard is paved with an undulating marble mosaic. A favourite for the evening stroll (or *paseo*). *Map U3*

3 MARQ (Museo Arqueológico Provincial de Alicante)
A hi-tech, hands-on museum with plenty of multimedia gadgets. Educational and hugely entertaining. *Plaza Dr Gómez Ulla s/n • Map V1 • 965 14 90 06 • Open winter: 10am–7pm Tue–Sat, 10am–2pm Sun & public hols; summer: call ahead for details • www.marqalicante.com • Adm charge*

4 Ayuntamiento
Alicante's town hall is the city's finest Baroque building. *Plaza de Ayuntamiento • Map U2 • 965 14 91 00 • Open 9am–2pm Mon–Fri • Free*

Barrio de Santa Cruz

5 Barrio de Santa Cruz
Alicante's oldest quarter – a chaotic tumble of whitewashed houses, crooked stairways, and flower-filled balconies. *Map U2*

6 Basílica de Santa María
Alicante's oldest and prettiest church. *Plaza de Santa María • Map V2 • 965 21 60 26 • Open during religious services • Free*

7 Concatedral de San Nicolás
The hulking 17th-century cathedral dominates the old quarter. *C/Labradores • Map U2 • 965 21 26 62 • Open during religious services • Free*

8 Lucentum
In Roman times, Lucentum was a sizeable trading centre. All that remains are these evocative ruins on a small mound by the sea. *C/Zeus, Playa de la Albufereta • Map V2 • 965 14 90 06 • Open 10am–2pm, 4–6pm Tue–Sat, 10am–2pm Sun; Jul & Aug: call ahead for details • www.marqalicante.com • Adm charge*

9 Alicante Port
An entertainment centre has added more shops and a cinema to this hive of activity. *Map U3*

10 Monasterio de la Santa Faz
A pilgrimage to this monastery 8 km (5 miles) from the city centre takes place on the second Thursday after Easter Sunday. *Ctra de Valencia • Map V1 • 965 26 49 12 • Open during religious services*

Las Hogueras de San Juan

The fabulous fiery festival of Las Hogueras (Fogueres in Valenciano), the biggest on the Alicante calendar, culminates on midsummer day, 24 June, the feast day of St John the Baptist. It begins with a bang – literally – on 20 June, with "La Mascletà", an ear-splitting barrage of firecrackers. Each neighbourhood vies to create the best hoguera, *an enormous figure of wax or papier mâché. At midnight on the 24th, after a spectacular fireworks display from the top of the castle, all the* hogueras *are set on fire – even the winning entry. There are folk parades, bullfights, medieval markets and firecracker competitions throughout the week.*

The Hogueras

The *hogueras* are huge, colourful and elaborate. Each one can take as long as a year to build – and yet all will go up in flames. Only one piece of a *hoguera* (not necessarily from the winning entry and known as the "*Ninot Indultat*") will not suffer this fate.

Fireworks display at the Festival of San Juan in Alicante, Spain

Top 10 Other Festivals in Alicante

1. Various dates all year: Moros y Cristianos (mock battles)
2. Mid-Jan: Porrate de San Antón (traditional fair)
3. Feb: Carnavales (Carnival)
4. Easter: Semana Santa (Holy Week)
5. Second Thu after Easter Sunday: Peregrinación de la Santa Faz (pilgrimage)
6. May: Cruces de Mayo (flower competition)
7. Jul, Aug: Fiestas de Verano (music, dance, theatre)
8. 16 July: Virgen del Carmen (sailor's festival)
9. 3 Aug: Virgen del Remedio (dedicated to one of Alicante's patron saints)
10. 6 Dec: Fiesta de San Nicólas (another patron saint of the city)

Guadalest

The tiny village of Guadalest is a spectacular sight, perched precariously on a lofty crag and topped by the ruins of a medieval castle. Its picture-postcard charm draws crowds of day-trippers, yet Guadalest has managed to keep its medieval allure. The upper village is accessed by a tunnel hewn through the rock; beneath is the chaotic sprawl of the old Muslim quarter, with a souk-like string of souvenir shops and cafés. The view from the castle walls at the very summit of the village extends all the way down to the coast.

View of Guadalest

There are plenty of cafés in the Plaza San Gregorio (upper village). The best restaurant in the area is Venta la Montaña, in Benimantell, 1 km (half a mile) from Guadalest (Ctra Alcoi 9. 96 588 5141) serving traditional local specialities. It is closed on Mondays.

- *Map F3*
- *Tourist office: Avda de Alicante s/n. 965 88 52 98. Open 11:30am–2pm, 3–6:30pm Mon–Fri, 11am–1:30pm Sat (11am–2pm, 3–7pm Sun in summer)*
- *Casa Orduña: C/Iglesia 2. 965 88 53 93. Open summer: 10:30am–7:30pm daily; winter: 10:30am–5:30pm daily. Admission: €4 (includes castle entrance)*
- *Casa Tipica: C/Iglesia 1. 965 88 52 38. Open 10am–7pm (until 6pm in winter) Sun–Fri. Free (donation requested)*
- *Museo Microminiatura: C/Iglesia 5. 965 88 50 62. Open 10am–7pm Tue–Sun. Admission: €4*

Top 10 Features

1. Puerta de San José
2. Bell Tower
3. Castillo de San José
4. Casa Orduña
5. Cemetery
6. Plaza de San Gregorio
7. Casa Típica (Museo Etnológico)
8. Museo Microminiatura
9. Gifts and Souvenirs
10. Embalse de Guadalest

1 Puerta de San José

The entrance *(puerta)* to the upper village is a miniature whitewashed arch leading to a tunnel hollowed out of the rock. Pass through, and you emerge, in fairytale style, onto a cobbled street.

2 Bell Tower

The whitewashed bell tower has become a much-loved symbol of Guadalest *(below)*. From high above the village, its sweet, low chimes echo across the valley.

3 Castillo de San José

Almost nothing survives of the medieval castle, but the romantic ruins offer superb views of the surrounding countryside. Entrance is via the Casa Orduña, where a stone path culminates in the battered towers of the original fortress.

4 Casa Orduña

The grandest house in Guadalest, this imposing residence, once home to the Orduña family, seems to cling onto the cliff face. It still retains many of its original 18th- and 19th-century furnishings, paintings and *objets d'art*. The upper levels contain an art gallery.

Guadalest's tourist office overlooks the main parking area on the edge of the village.

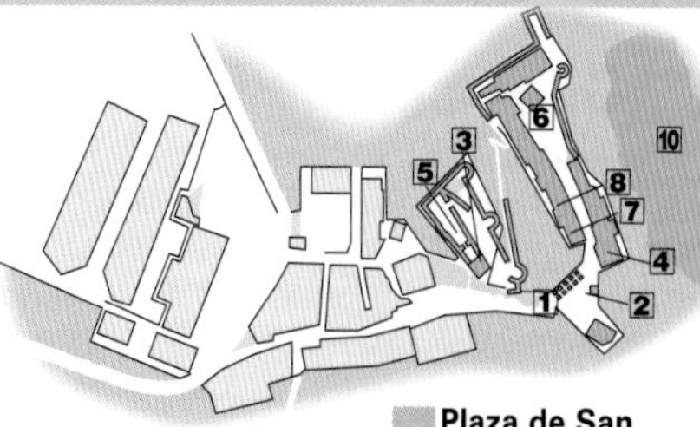

5 Cemetery

High up in the village is a tiny, neglected cemetery – the highest in Spain. It's scattered with a motley collection of limbless statues, and offers more breathtaking views over the valley. A bell-topped archway leads to the remnants of the castle walls.

6 Plaza de San Gregorio

The only street in the upper village leads to the Plaza San Gregorio, with a few shops, a cluster of cafés, and a spectacular viewing point *(mirador)* overlooking the beautiful reservoir below.

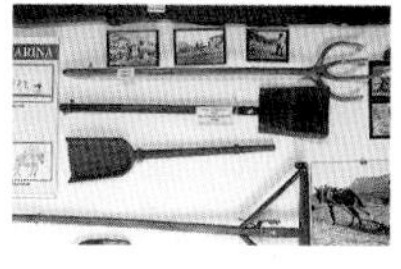

7 Casa Típica

Take a glimpse into Guadalest's domestic and agricultural past in this reconstruction of a typical late-18th-century farmhouse complete with tools, costumes, scale models of farm equipment and much more.

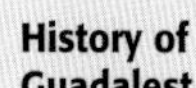

8 Museo Microminiatura

Guadalest is stuffed full of quirky museums; the Museo Microminiatura is one of the most curious. Its treasures are viewed through magnifying glasses, and include the Eiffel Tower sculpted on the head of a pin, and Velázquez's famous *Las Meninas* reproduced on a grain of corn.

9 Gifts and Souvenirs

Guadalest is crammed with gift shops, selling handmade lace, a range of honeys, fiery local spirits, and the usual tat.

10 Embalse de Guadalest

This vast reservoir *(embalse)* provides water for the parched coastal regions. It's also the perfect spot for a picnic *(right)*.

History of Guadalest

It's hard to imagine quaint little Guadalest as an important military outpost, yet for centuries it was just that. First built by the Arabs around 715, the castle was conquered and expanded by the Christian armies under Jaime I in 1238. Only natural disaster could topple it; during the great earthquake of 1644, the castle foundations were fatally damaged, and when another one hit in 1748, the entire edifice came tumbling down.

Guadalest is a popular coach trip from Benidorm. Get there as early as you can to beat the crowds, and try to avoid it altogether in high season.

Top 10 Penyal d'Ifac (Peñón de Ifach)

This sheer, impregnable crag dominating the bay of Calp (Calpe) has become the symbol of the Costa Blanca. Once a notorious pirate hideout, it's now a protected Natural Park perfumed with lavender and wild flowers. A steep trail zig-zags upward, burrows through a tunnel cut in the rock, then winds dramatically to a viewing point at the very summit, 332 m (1,089 ft) above sea level. A word of caution: the first section of the trail is suitable for walkers of all levels; after the tunnel, it becomes increasingly tricky.

View from a mirador

There are no cafés on the rock, but picnics are permitted so long as you collect all your rubbish. The nearby port has several cafés.

The number of visitors on the rock is strictly limited, with a maximum of 150 allowed to climb it at one time. In high season, get there early in the day, and try to avoid weekends if you want to avoid the queues.

The information centre is located at the park entrance.

- *Calp (Calpe)*
- *Map G4*
- *Visitor information centre: C/Illa de Formentera s/n. 965 83 75 96*
- *Open 8:30am–2:30pm Mon–Fri, 9:30am–2:30pm Sat, Sun (mid-Sep–May: 3:30–5:30pm Tue, Thu also)*
- *Free*

Top 10 Features

1. Hiking Trail
2. Tunnel
3. Summit of Ifac
4. Miradors
5. Climbing Routes
6. Flora and Fauna
7. Birds
8. Exhibition
9. Coves and Inlets
10. Port

1 Hiking Trail

On the lower flanks of the rock, the main trail to the summit twists and turns through gnarled pine trees and swathes of perfumed lavender. On the upper reaches, you'll need a head for heights and sturdy footwear.

2 Tunnel

In 1918, a tunnel was hacked through the rock to make the ascent easier. The floor here is steep and slippery, but at least visitors no longer have to be hauled over the cliff face by ropes, as was the old custom.

3 Summit of Ifac

The narrow hiking trail leads to the very summit of the rock, with stunning views of distant mountain ranges, the coastline and far out to sea.

4 Miradors

There are several viewing points *(miradors)* along the way, but the best views (besides those from the summit) are probably from the old guard post on the southern flank.

If you intend to follow the trail right to the summit, ensure that you have suitable footwear and plenty of water.

5 Climbing Routes

The Penyal d'Ifac is a rock-climbers' mecca. There are several climbing routes on both the north and south faces, which take between five and eleven hours.

6 Flora and Fauna

There are more than 300 species of flora on the scrubby slopes of Ifac, including lavender, golden rod, red valerian and St Bernard's lily. The rarest endemic plants are contained in two microreserves. Few animals besides lizards and other reptiles can survive in these rather parched conditions.

7 Birds

The Penyal d'Ifac is home to more than 80 species of bird, including Eleanora's falcon, the peregrine falcon, the shag and the northern gannet. There are several species of gull, including the yellow-legged gull and the rarer Audoin's gull.

8 Exhibition

A cluster of buildings at the base of the Penyal d'Ifac contains the park information office and two exhibition rooms, which highlight the most important features of the park and describe the wildlife to be found within its borders.

9 Coves and Inlets

The base of the Penyal d'Ifac is dotted with picturesque coves, which also have protected status under the Natural Park scheme. A paradise for divers and snorkellers, the crystal-clear waters are home to a wealth of marine life.

10 Port

Calp's port sits at the neck of the narrow isthmus which joins the Penyal d'Ifac with the mainland. It's a cheerful mixture of sleek yachts and battered fishing boats. Cafés and ice-cream parlours aplenty offer welcome refreshment after an exhausting climb.

The Penyal Underwater

The Penyal d'Ifac is as fascinating under water as it is above; octopuses and scorpion fish lurk in the shadows, and dive-through tunnels are encrusted with colourful anemones. Several companies in the area offer beginners' diving courses, as well as dives around the rock. These include Club Nautico Les Basetes (Ctra Calpe-Moraira Km 2, Benissa; 965 83 54 28) and Dive & Dive (Avda del Port 14, Calp; 965 83 92 70 or 670 61 32 61; www.divedivecompany.com).

The Penyal d'Ifac has been one of the Costa Blanca's major tourist attractions for decades.

TOP 10 Casa-Museo Modernista, Novelda

Anyone who has seen Gaudí's buildings in Barcelona will love this lavish Art Nouveau-style town house, crammed with swirling woodwork, delicate wrought iron and turn-of-the-20th-century furnishings. It belonged to Antonia Navarro, a young widow with a substantial fortune, and was designed by the celebrated Murcian architect Pedro Cerdán. It fell into disrepair after the Civil War, but a meticulous restoration project has returned the graceful salons to their former glory.

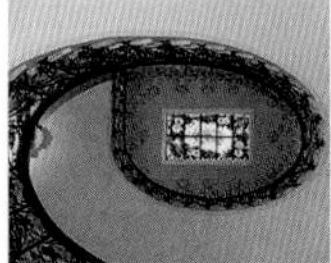

Skylight over stairwell

There is no café in the building, but you can enjoy local delicacies at the Nou Cucuch restaurant and tapas bar on C/Pasaje Isidro Seller 8 (965 60 15 00; open Fri, Sat, Sun L).

The building has no lift, and wheelchair access is limited.

Fans of Modernista architecture should also visit Novelda's Casino on C/Emilio Castelar s/n (965 60 00 30), and St Mary Magdalene's Sanctuary, 3 km (2 miles) from Novelda on Cerro de la Mola.

- *C/Mayor 24, Novelda*
- *Map D5*
- *965 60 02 37*
- *Open 10am–2pm Tue–Sat (also in the afternoon in winter; call for more details)*
- *Free*
- *Novelda tourist information office: C/Mayor 6. 965 60 92 28*

Top 10 Features

1. Façade
2. Study
3. Dining Room
4. Patio/Courtyard
5. Staircase
6. Stained-glass Ceilings
7. Gallery
8. Ballroom
9. Bedrooms
10. Exhibitions

1 Façade

The façade fuses Classical lines and Modernista details: curvaceous wrought-iron balconies; a profusion of stone fruit and flowers; an intricately carved door flanked with rosy marble panels.

2 Study

The study is full of exquisitely carved woodwork, from the sculpted leaves on the fireplace to the undulating panelling on the lower walls *(right)*.

3 Dining Room

This lavish room *(above)* contains frescoes of languid women in woodland settings, elaborately trimmed doorways, and richly carved furniture.

In the study, look out for the corner cupboard in the form of a stalactite-filled grotto.

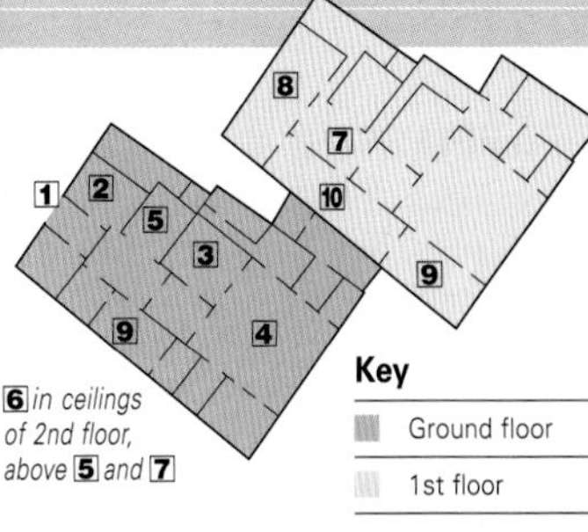

4 Patio/Courtyard

The delightful, ivy-draped patio is lined with pale sculpted columns supporting delicate arches. Hand-painted tiles depict Antonia Navarro's substantial country estates.

5 Staircase

The marble staircase curves sinuously upward, an intricate garland of wrought-iron vine tendrils curling between the balusters. Carved wooden panels succeed each other like waves. The bannister culminates in a graceful lamp *(below)*.

6 Stained-glass Ceilings

The entrance hall is flooded with light from a spectacular stained-glass ceiling of multicoloured flowers and leaves. Over the stairwell, a smaller, even more extravagant stained-glass ceiling is surrounded by ceramic flowers and exuberant plasterwork.

7 Gallery

The exceptional woodwork featured throughout the house reaches its apotheosis in the sumptuous wooden gallery which encloses the stairwell. Loops and swirls of burnished walnut are richly carved with intricate detailing.

8 Ballroom

The ballroom is a theatrical whirl of red and gold. The exquisite tiled floor *(right)* was designed by Catalan architect Domenech i Montaner.

9 Bedrooms

All of the bedrooms have original furnishings. The bathroom adjoining the main bedroom has a huge bath carved from a single slab of marble.

10 Exhibitions

The house has two permanent exhibitions: one of Art Nouveau-style graphic design; the other dedicated to Novelda-born explorer Jorge Juan.

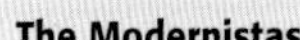

The Modernistas

Modernista architecture is characterized by organic forms, flowing lines and elaborate decoration. It celebrated the traditional crafts of woodcarving, stone-masonry and ceramic tiling, but used them in entirely new ways. The most famous Modernista architect was Gaudí. His spellbinding buildings in Barcelona, now world-famous, influenced many architects in the Costa Blanca region, who incorporated his dazzling use of colour and revolutionary sense of form into their beautiful new mansions and public buildings.

Sierra de Espuña

The verdant, pine-clad mountain range of the Sierra de Espuña erupts magically from the parched Murcian plain. A Regional Park since 1995, it's criss-crossed with spectacular walking and mountain-biking trails, with some tougher hikes across the peaks. To the east lie the "bad lands", an unearthly swathe of arid hills and abrupt canyons, which contrast dramatically with the luxuriance of the mountain forests. Scattered across the northern flanks of the Sierra de Espuña are the ancient snow wells, picturesque ruins deep in the pine forest.

View from park entrance

Fuente del Hilo, an inexpensive café-restaurant near the visitor information centre, serves good grilled local meat and fish (968 43 92 23; closed Mon, Tue and whole of Aug).

There are three camping areas and, for serious hikers, four mountain refuges in the park *(see p131)*. The Visitors Centre has lists of hotels, *pensiones* and *casas rurales* in the region.

- *Map L3*
- *Visitor information centre (Centro Ricardo Cordorniú): Parque Regional Sierra Espuña. 968 43 14 30. www.sierraespuna.com Open 10am–2pm, 3–6pm Tue–Sun and bank holidays*
- *Park refuge booking line: 968 22 88 29*
- *Free*

Top 10 Features

1. Visitors Centre
2. Pozos de Nieve
3. Barrancos de Gebas
4. Birds
5. Peaks
6. Flora and Fauna
7. Drive
8. Walking Trails
9. Miradors
10. Alhama de Murcia

1 Visitors Centre

This handsomely restored building *(above)* contains a small but lively exhibition geared toward children, outlining the park's history and the wildlife to be found within its borders. An information desk has maps and leaflets describing walking trails.

2 Pozos de Nieve

These strange, circular brick huts were used to store snow, which was packed into ice, and transported by donkey to the towns to make ice cream. They were used from the 16th century right up until the 1920s *(right)*.

3 Barrancos de Gebas

Tacked onto the eastern end of the Sierra Espuña is the strange lunar landscape of the Barrancos de Gebas, known as the "bad lands" *(tierras malas)*, where the lushness of the sierra gives way to a startling succession of arid ravines and gullies.

The closest tourist information office is in Alhama de Murcia.

4 Birds

The park is rich in bird life, particularly raptors, among them golden, booted and Bonelli's eagles, eagle and tawny owls, peregrine falcon, Dupont's lark, goshawk and hawk owl.

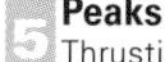

5 Peaks

Thrusting up through forest, the stony peaks of the Sierra de Espuña *(left)* are a glorious sight. At 1,583 m (5,194 ft), Espuña is the highest. Pedro López (1,507 m; 4,944 ft) is also magnificent.

6 Flora and Fauna

The indigenous forest has been substantially supplemented by pine. You may well see wild sheep, squirrels, bats and wild boars; mountain cats are less common.

7 Drive

The drive through the park is extraordinary; the road twists up through the Collado Bermejo, offering a staggering panorama of jutting crags and plunging valleys, then down again through flower-strewn woodland to the Visitors Centre.

8 Walking Trails

The park is full of excellent walking trails geared toward walkers of all levels. Choose from simple woodland paths suitable for families to tougher hikes across the peaks. The information points provide maps and leaflets on the trails.

9 Miradors

Throughout the park there is a series of *miradors* (viewing points) which offer staggering views over peaks, forest and riverbeds. The finest views are from Espuña and the Morrón Chico.

10 Alhama de Murcia

Alhama de Murcia is not the most charming town in the area, but it's the easiest access point for the Sierra Espuña, and a good place to buy picnic supplies or find a hotel.

Park Guide

The best way to approach the Sierra Espuña is from Alhama de Murcia, as this road passes the visitors centre, where you can pick up maps and get information on the various walking trails. The snow wells can be found in the northwest section of the park; take the road signposted *pozos de nieve* from the Collado Bermejo viewing point, and walk down the gravel path near the small (unmarked) car park.

Rarer residents of the forest include the Pseudohadana mariana *butterfly.*

TOP 10 Hort del Cura, Elx (Elche)

Elx, a tranquil city at the centre of a vast plain, is surrounded by a glorious palm grove, first established by the Phoenicians in the 7th century BC and today a UNESCO World Heritage Site. In the most spectacular corner of this grove is the Hort del Cura (Priest's Garden), with more than 700 palms and a blaze of brilliant blooms around a restful pond. First laid out in its current form in the 19th century by Don José Castaño (the priest after whom the garden is named), the garden achieved international fame in the 1940s under Juan Orts Román.

Cactus Garden

There is a kiosk selling drinks and snacks within the garden. For a smart lunch, head to the elegant hotel Huerto del Cura directly opposite the garden ***(see p124)*****.**

The gardens are small, and best visited early in the morning or late in the evening, when there are fewer crowds. Come out of season if you can, and try to avoid weekends. There is a useful audioguide.

- *Porta de la Morera 49*
- *Map D6, Q1*
- *965 45 19 36*
- *www.huertodelcura.com*
- *Open 9am–6pm daily (Mar–Jun: to 8pm; Jul, Aug: to 9pm; Sep, Oct: to 7pm)*
- *Admission €5 inclusive of autoguide (children €2.50)*
- *Elx tourist office: Plaza del Parque 3. 966 65 81 96. Open 9am–7pm Mon–Fri, 10am–7pm Sat, 10am–2pm Sun, hols*

Top 10 Features

1. Imperial Palm
2. Date Palms
3. Sculptures
4. Lily Pond
5. Rock Garden and Cactuses
6. Bust of Jaime I
7. La Casa
8. Chapel
9. Named Palms
10. Flowers

1 Imperial Palm

This magnificent palm *(below)* is almost 200 years old. Named in honour of a visit by the Empress of Austria in 1894, it has seven branches, like a huge candelabrum. It weighs around eight tonnes.

2 Date Palms

Most of the palms in Elx are date palms. The legend goes that they were brought here by the Phoenicians, who ate the dates on the long sea journey, then planted the stones.

3 Sculptures

The most dramatic sculpture in the park is by Alicantino artist Eusebi Sempere – a gently revolving circle of metal spikes that appears to shift shape as it turns *(below)*.

4 Lily Pond

Turtles bask and frogs chatter on the fringes of the pretty lily pond at the heart of the park *(main image)*. You can hop across it on a series of stepping stones.

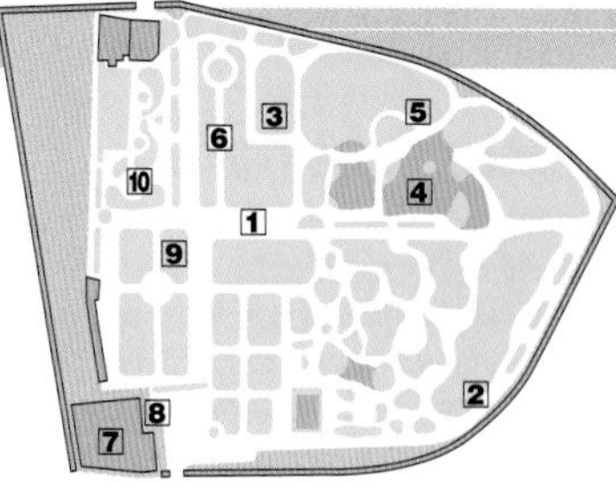

5 Rock Garden and Cactuses

Behind the pond, a tumble of rocks forms a Wild West-style backdrop to the cactus collection. There are tall, spiky varieties as big as trees, many sprouting scarlet fruit and flowers, as well as plump cactuses of the type known as "mother-in-law's cushion".

6 Bust of Jaime I

A small bust of King Jaime I sits at the western end of the park, commemorating the king's decision to save the palm groves of Elx from destruction after the city was taken from the Arabs in 1265.

7 La Casa

The simple house *(above)* at the entrance to the park was built in 1940, and incorporates palm trunks into its design. It holds administrative offices and isn't open to the public.

8 Chapel

A tiny chapel holds the remains of Juan Orts Román, who remodelled the gardens and ensured that they received international attention. Román was the son of the "Cura" after whom the gardens are named *(left)*.

9 Named Palms

Since 1900, a number of palms have been dedicated to distinguished people, and bear a small plaque. The dedicatees are sent the fruits of the tree during their lifetime.

10 Flowers

The garden is full of strelitzias *(below)*, better known as "birds of paradise" for their spiky forms and extraordinary colours. There's also a brilliant tumble of purple and red bougainvillea at the south-western end.

Elx Palms

About 95 per cent of the palms in Elx are date palms, which produce vast quantities of fruit. While some of the fruit is cultivated and sold, the most economically viable crop to come from the palms is the dried fronds. Elx is the main supplier of fronds to make crosses for use on Palm Sunday. The palm crosses are often kept all year long because they are popularly believed to ward off lightning.

Dedicatees of the garden's palms include pianist Arthur Rubinstein and Nobel Prize-winning scientist Severo Ochoa.

Isla Tabarca

Tabarca is the only inhabited island on the Alicante coast. The western end is wild and empty, guarded by an 18th-century watchtower and a remote lighthouse; at the eastern end is the pretty walled village of Nova Tabarca. The island's only sandy beach, with a cluster of busy seafood restaurants and cafés, backs onto the port. It can get very busy in summer, particularly at weekends. The incredibly clear waters which surround the island have been designated a marine reserve and are popular with divers and snorkellers.

South Gate

There are several cafés and restaurants in the port area, offering local specialities like *caldero tabarquino*, a delicious fish stew. Try the mid-range La Almadraba *(see p91)*.

The ferry service from Santa Pola (at least four crossings a day) is faster and more frequent than the one from Alicante (daily in summer, three times a week during the rest of the year).

For tourist information, consult the Santa Pola tourist office.

- *Map E6, R1*
- *Santa Pola tourist office: C/Astilleros 4. 966 69 60 52*

Top 10 Sights

1. Casa del Gobernador
2. Iglesia de San Pedro y San Pablo
3. Lighthouse
4. Torre de San José
5. Beach
6. Marine Reserve
7. Port
8. City Walls
9. The Islands
10. Nova Tabarca

1 Casa del Gobernador

Long since stripped of its original fittings, the 18th-century Governor's House *(above)* is undergoing major restoration work and will reopen as a hotel.

2 Iglesia de San Pedro y San Pablo

Dedicated to St Peter and St Paul, Tabarca's church, perched right above the sea, is built of faded, rosy stone. Its simple façade has some pretty Baroque flourishes.

3 Lighthouse

Tabarca's lighthouse *(below)* emerges from the scrubby wilderness at the western tip of the island. It is a substantial 19th-century affair combining sturdy living quarters with a slender tower. Long mechanized, the lighthouse is closed to visitors.

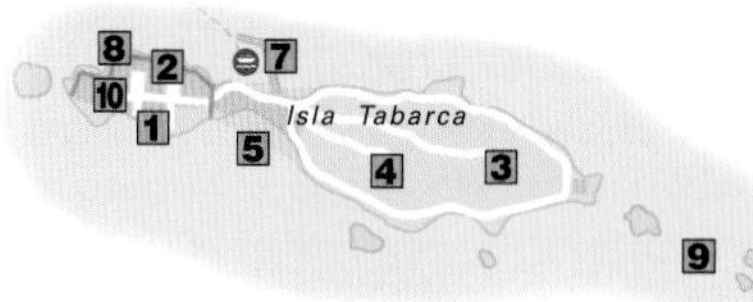

4 Torre de San José

This impressive 18th-century watchtower was built as part of the fortifications which protected the islanders from pirate raids. In the 19th century it was used as a prison.

5 Beach

The main beach on Tabarca is a silvery arc of sand opposite the port. It attracts huge numbers of sunbathers and swimmers during summer. Thanks to their shingle beaches, the gorgeous coves which fringe the entire island are less popular, so they make great places to escape the crowds.

6 Marine Reserve

The island of Tabarca was declared a marine reserve in 1986. Its waters contain a wealth of aquatic life among the rocks and reefs. A number of companies in Santa Pola offer diving and snorkelling trips.

7 Port

Tabarca's little port is the island's hub, where a few colourfully painted fishing boats are dwarfed by the incoming and outgoing ferries.

8 City Walls

The 18th-century village of Nova Tabarca was fortified to withstand pirate attacks. Stretches of wall and some of the gates survive *(above)*.

9 The Islands

Tabarca is the largest island of a small archipelago. The islets off its coast are perfect for swimming and picnicking.

10 Nova Tabarca

The quiet streets of this simple little settlement of low, brightly painted houses offer delightful glimpses of flower-filled patios and palm-shaded squares.

Pirates, Kings, and Islanders

In 1768, King Carlos III granted sanctuary to a group of largely Genoese prisoners who had been expelled from the original island of Tabarka, a Spanish possession off the coast of Tunisia. A walled town was built for the immigrants, who called their new home Nova Tabarca. This wasn't pure altruism on the King's part; the pirates who had long used the island as a base for coastal raids were forced to find new hideouts when the settlement was built.

Most of the smaller islands off the coast of Tabarca can be reached on foot by scrambling over the rocks – but watch the tide.

TOP 10 Palau Ducal, Gandia (Gandía)

This impressive Gothic palace with origins in the late 13th century was acquired by the Dukes of Borja – better known by their Italian name Borgia – in the late 15th. Expanded and embellished over the years, its most sumptuous apartments date from the late 18th century, when lavish Baroque salons dripping with gold leaf were added. Famous for the shimmering ceramic tiles which adorn its walls, galleries and balconies, the palace has been immaculately restored by its current owners, the Jesuits.

Decorative azulejos

The palace has no café. The Santanjordi restaurant nearby offers contemporary Mediterranean fare with an eastern twist, at a medium price (Paseo Germanías 36; 962 87 81 77; closed Sun D, Mon).

Full access to the palace is by guided tour only. Tours are given exclusively in either Spanish or Valencian. It's worth calling in advance to ensure that the multimedia exhibit can be heard in your language.

- *C/Duc Alfons el Vell 1*
- *Map F2*
- *962 87 14 65*
- *www.palauducal.com*
- *Open 10am–2pm, 4–8pm (winter: 3–7pm) Tue–Sat, 10am–2pm Sun. Guided tours are available throughout the day*
- *Admission €6*

Top 10 Features

1. Main Façade
2. Entrance Hall
3. Exhibition
4. Patio de Armas
5. Salón de Águilas
6. Galería Dorada
7. Mosaic of the Four Elements
8. Salón de Coronas
9. Chapel
10. Oratory

1 Main Façade

The simple stone façade, a sober Gothic portal topped with a faded coat of arms and flanked by narrow windows, gives no hint of the luxury within. Only its scale reveals the grandeur of the family that once lived here.

2 Entrance Hall

Nothing survives of the 13th-century palace but the entrance hall which leads to the central patio. The beamed ceiling is original; its painted decoration has faded over the centuries.

3 Exhibition

The history of the palace and the story of the Borja family are recounted in a fun multimedia exhibition at the beginning of the tour. Note the glowing *azulejos* (tiles) which adorn the walls of the projection room – there are even finer tiles within the palace itself.

4 Patio de Armas

The Patio de Armas *(left)* is the main courtyard of the former palace. Once it would have rung with the clatter of carriages making for the stables at its northeastern corner

While the Borgias were engaged in a variety of nefarious activities, the Borjas produced a saint, Francis of Borja.

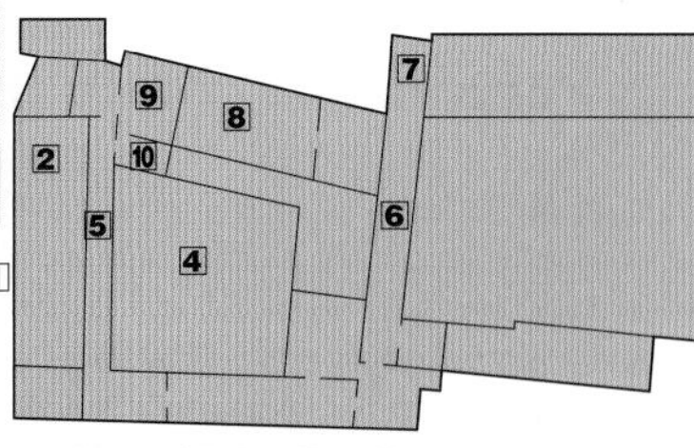

1st floor of Palau Ducal *(3 on ground floor)*

5 Salón de Águilas

This extravagantly decorated 18th-century hall boasts a dazzling gilded frieze of fierce eagles *(águilas)* feasting on clumps of fruit.

6 Galería Dorada

The sumptuous 18th-century Galería Dorada *(left)*, a succession of apartments opening into one long hall, is a breath-taking whirl of gilded stucco and colourful tiles.

7 The Four Elements

The Galería Dorada culminates in a stunning mosaic representing the four elements; the sun (Fire) is encircled by birds and butterflies (Air), fish and boats (Water), and plants and flowers (Earth).

8 Salón de Coronas

The majestic 16th-century Hall of Crowns *(left)* takes its name from the crowns that decorate the elaborate wooden ceiling. One of the building's oldest windows can be found in this room.

9 Chapel

A brilliant blue vaulted ceiling scattered with golden stars soars above the Neo-Gothic chapel, created in the room that was formerly St Francis of Borja's office.

10 Oratory

A simple chapel next to the saint's humble bedroom was transformed in the 19th century into this splendidly decorated miniature oratory with a series of murals and an exquisite marquetry floor.

St Francis of Borja (1510–72)

Francis of Borja was a close advisor to Carlos I of Spain at the time of the queen's death in 1539. Asked to escort her remains for burial in Granada, Francis was so appalled at the sight of her decomposed body that he immediately announced his intention to "follow a master who cannot die" and abandoned the court for a simple religious life. He joined the Jesuits in 1548, and was finally canonized in 1670.

The bed in which St Francis of Borja reputedly slept is in the Salón de Águilas, tucked behind some neo-Gothic arches.

TOP 10 Catedral de Santa María, Murcia

The Cathedral of Santa María looms proudly over the centre of Murcia. The finest Baroque building in a city overflowing with Baroque architecture, it also contains some spectacular examples of the Gothic and Renaissance styles. The first stone was laid on the site of a former Arab mosque in 1394, and the first mass was celebrated in the mid-15th century. The richly ornamented façade, with Corinthian columns, stone swoops and curves, and a dazzling array of sculpted saints, was built in the 18th century.

The spectacular 19th-century organ, seen from the Choir.

A short walk from the cathedral, Los Zagales (C/Polo de Medina 4; 968 21 55 79) is a great place for tapas, with a crowd of locals permanently propping up the bar. The walls are covered with photos of famous footballers and bullfighters. Closed Sundays.

Bring some €1 coins to illuminate the highlights of the cathedral interior, including the Choir, the Capilla de los Vélez and the Capilla del Junterón.

- *Plaza del Cardenal Belluga*
- *Map U6, N3*
- *968 21 63 44*
- *Open: 7am–1pm, 6–8pm (winter: 5–8pm) daily*
- *Free*

Top 10 Features

1. Baroque Façade
2. Puerta de los Apóstoles
3. Puerta del Perdón
4. Coro
5. Capilla de los Vélez
6. Capilla del Junterón
7. Puerta de la Sacristía
8. Altar Mayor
9. Museo Catedralicio
10. Bell Tower

1 Baroque Façade

The spectacular main façade *(right)*, with its ranks of Corinthian columns and lavishly carved stonework, was built from 1739–54 by architect Jaime Bort. It overlooks the lovely Plaza del Cardenal Belluga.

2 Puerta de los Apóstoles

The elaborate Gothic portal on the southern side of the cathedral *(above)* is set in a sea of sculpture, including images of the four apostles and a cloud of angelic musicians. Queen Isabella's coat of arms crowns the portal – she gave generously toward the cathedral's construction.

3 Puerta del Perdón

Surmounted by an exquisite sculpture of the Virgin Mary with angels, the central doorway of the main façade was once reserved for royalty.

4 Coro

The sumptuous stalls in the Gothic choir *(below)* are densely carved with biblical scenes.

A faded casket behind the main altar contains the heart of the medieval king Alfonso X the Wise.

5 Capilla de los Vélez

The jewel of the cathedral is the Capilla de los Vélez, the magnificent late 15th-century burial place of the powerful Marquises of Vélez. Look out for the "noble savages" – a fashionable motif after Columbus's voyage to the Americas.

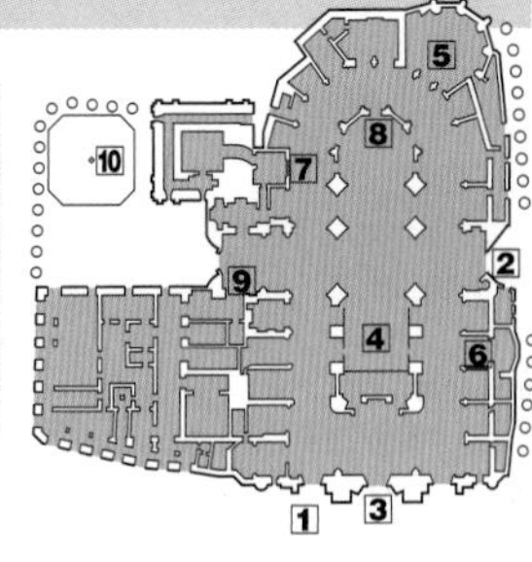

6 Capilla del Junterón

This dazzling chapel (another aristocratic burial place) is the grandest expression of Renaissance architecture in Murcia. Adorned with graceful saints and Classical figures, it contains a shimmering 16th-century altarpiece topped by a truly spectacular relief.

7 Puerta de la Sacristía

Baroque at its most flamboyant, this extravagant doorway is in the form of a splendid triumphal arch, with columns and pedestals supporting a host of cherubs surmounted by the three Virtues.

8 Altar Mayor

The vast main altarpiece *(left)* was partially rebuilt in 1862 by a Yecla sculptor. It forms an impressive golden wall behind the main altar.

9 Museo Catedralicio

The newly expanded cathedral museum houses paintings, sculpture and ceremonial objects, including an extraordinary Baroque silver monstrance.

10 Bell Tower

The delightful bell tower, with its Baroque frills and flounces, is an oddly harmonious mish-mash of styles *(right)*.

The Bell Tower

Work started on the cathedral bell tower in 1519, but it was not completed until 1793. Each of its five levels is in a different style. Beginning with a theatrically Gothic section complete with swarms of fabulous creatures, the tower ascends to a winsome Baroque lantern right at the very top. You could once get a close-up look at the changing architectural styles by climbing the belltower, but, sadly, it is now closed to visitors.

In the cathedral museum, look out for a haunting 14th-century altarpiece and an extraordinary solid silver Baroque monstrance.

Left **Plazas Las Flores and Santa Catalina** Centre **Casino de Murcia** Right **Museo Salzillo**

Other Sights in Murcia

1 Casino de Murcia

Murcia's Modernista casino is a hotchpotch of styles, with an Arabic vestibule, a Rococo ballroom, and a Neo-Classical salon. *C/Trapería 18 • Map U5 • 968 21 22 55 • Closed for restoration • www.casinomurcia.com • Adm charge*

2 Museo Salzillo

A museum devoted to the work of Francisco Salzillo *(see p54)*. *Plaza San Agustín 3 • Map S5 • 968 29 18 93 • Open summer: 10am–2pm, 5–8 pm Tue–Fri, 10am–2pm Sat; winter: 10am–2pm, 5–8pm Tue–Sat, 11am–2pm Sun • www.museosalzillo.es • Adm charge*

3 Museo de la Ciencia y el Agua

A delightful, fun-filled museum, with interactive exhibits, models and even a tiny planetarium. *Plaza de la Ciencia 1 • Map T6 • 968 21 19 98 • Open summer: 10am–2pm, 5–8pm Mon–Fri; winter: 10am–2pm, 5–8pm Tue–Sat, 11am–2pm Sun • www.cienciayagua.org • Adm charge*

4 Iglesia de la Merced

The graceful former Convent of Mercy is now part of the university complex. *C/Santo Cristo 2 • Map U5 • Open for Mass only*

Museo Hidráulico Los Molinos

5 Museo de Bellas Artes

There are almost 1,000 paintings on display at the Fine Arts Museum, mainly by Murcian artists. *C/Obispo Frutos 12 • Map V5 • 968 23 93 46 • 10am–8:30pm Tue–Sat, 10am–2pm Sun • Free*

6 Museo Hidráulico Los Molinos del Río Segura

A fascinating museum dedicated to the watermills that once lined the River Segura. *C/Molinos 1 • Map T6 • 968 35 86 00 • Open 10am–2pm, 5–8pm Mon–Sat (Sat closed in summer) • www.molinosdelrio.org • Free*

7 Plazas Las Flores and Santa Catalina

The prettiest and liveliest of all Murcia's café-squares. *Map T5*

8 Teatro Romea

Murcia's main venue for the performing arts, along with the Auditorium and the Congress Centre. *Plaza Julián Romea s/n • Map T5 • 968 35 53 90 • www.teatroromea.org*

9 Mercado de las Verónicas

There's nowhere better to appreciate the wealth and variety of Murcian produce than this lively covered market. *Map T6*

10 Santuario de Nuestra Señora de la Fuensanta

High on a steep crag, this 16th-century sanctuary is dedicated to the patron saint of Murcia. *Algezares (5 km/3 miles from Murcia) • Map V6 • 968 84 22 01 • Open 9am–1pm, 4–6:30pm daily • Free*

Top 10 Famous Murcians

1. Ben Arabí (1164–1240) – philosopher
2. Diego Saavedra Fajardo (1584–1648) – diplomat and politician
3. José Moñino Redondo, Count of Floridablanca (1728–1808) – politician and intellectual
4. Julián Romea (1813–1868) – actor
5. Isaac Peral (1851–1895) – submarine inventor
6. Vicente Medina Tomás (1866–1937) – writer and poet
7. Juan de la Cierva (1895–1936) – inventor of the *autogiro*, an early helicopter
8. Carmen Conde (1907–1996) – poet, novelist and essayist
9. Narciso Yepes (1927–1997) – classical guitarist
10. Paco Rabal (1926–2001) – film star

Francisco Salzillo (1707–1783)

The Baroque sculptor Francisco Salzillo is Murcia's favourite son. He took naturalism to new heights with his emotionally charged sculptures. Every detail – from frown lines to fingernails – is meticulously carved, creating extraordinarily lifelike figures. Salzillo's fame spread rapidly during his lifetime, but he hated travelling and refused all invitations to court, never leaving Murcia if he could help it. His most celebrated works adorn the elaborate pasos *(floats) still used in Murcia's Holy Week processions.*

El Prendimiento (The Arrest), 1765

Part of a larger sculptural group, Salzillo's depiction of Judas's betrayal of Christ in the Garden of Gethsemane is extremely powerful. The two figures are carved from a single piece of wood.

Salzillo float during a Holy Week procession

INFORMACION
La Vida Loca
A

Left *The Fall of Granada* by C. L. Ribera y Fieve Right Jaime II of Aragón (19th-century etching)

Top 10 Moments in History

1 c.50000 BC–c.1000 BC: Prehistory

The Costa Blanca has been inhabited since Paleolithic times, with cave dwellers living in the inland hills from around 50000 BC. Iberian settlements began to appear around 3000 BC. Later, two Bronze Age cultures emerged: Argaric in the south and Valencian in the north.

2 c.1000 BC–c.200BC: Phoenicians, Greeks and Carthaginians

By 1000 BC, the Phoenicians and the Greeks were establishing trading settlements along the coast. The Carthaginians, landless after their defeat in the First Punic War, established Cartago Nova (modern Cartagena) in the 3rd century BC.

3 c.200 BC–c. AD 400: Romans

Rome crushed Carthage in the Second Punic War, marking the beginning of Roman domination of the Iberian Peninsula. The Romans brought with them their laws, their language and their roads, and established important settlements at Denia (Dénia), Alicante (Alacant) and Cartagena.

4 c.400–711: Visigoths

By the middle of the 4th century AD, the Roman Empire had splintered, and the Iberian Peninsula was invaded by a succession of northern tribes. The Visigoths arrived in 411 and eventually took control of most of Spain, but dynastic disputes left them ripe for conquest by the next wave of invaders.

5 711–c.1200: Arabs

In 711, the first Berber armies invaded the Iberian Peninsula, conquering most of it within a decade. Renamed Al-Andalus, it was ruled first by a mighty caliphate and then as a series of smaller kingdoms *(taifas)*. Arabic irrigation techniques created the fertile orchards which still characterize the Costa Blanca.

6 c.1200–c.1300: The Reconquista

Pockets of northern Spain remained resistant to the Arab armies, and it was from here that the Christian Reconquest was launched. Battles raged through much of the 13th century. Mursiya (Murcia) was taken by Jaime I of Aragón in 1266; Al Lekant (Alicante) fell to Jaime II in 1296.

Ruined Roman theatre, Cartagena

Preceding pages **Alicante harbour by night**

7 1244–c.1700: The Kingdom of Valencia

After the Reconquest, Jaime I re-established the Kingdom of Valencia, with special privileges, including the right to a separate court and their own currency. These ancient rights were only withdrawn after the Kingdom backed the losing side in the War of the Succession (1700–1714).

8 1244–c.1700: Murcia on the Frontier

In 1244, Murcia, strategically located on the border with the Arabic kingdom of Granada, became a vassal state of the powerful Kingdom of Castile, which annexed it outright in 1266. When Granada fell in 1492, Muslim converts *(Moriscos)* flooded into Murcia. Their expulsion in the early 17th century caused economic crisis.

9 The Lost Years (1700–1939)

Spain suffered during the wars and political upheavals of the 18th and 19th centuries. However, much of the region's most spectacular architecture was built during intermittent periods of prosperity. Simmering unrest in the early years of the 20th century erupted into the bloody Civil War (1936–9), won by General Franco.

10 Since 1939

Regional differences – including the Valencian language – were savagely suppressed under Franco's dictatorship. The advent of mass tourism in the 1960s brought jobs, money and a swathe of new development. Franco died in 1975, and democracy was peacefully restored. Tourism continues to provide the Costa Blanca with most of its wealth.

Top 10 Historical Figures

1 Dama de Elx (4th century BC)
Historical or mythical? – no one knows. The origins of this exquisite Iberian sculpture are shrouded in mystery *(see p83)*.

2 Hannibal Barca (c.247–c.183 BC)
The Carthaginian general who famously crossed the Alps with elephants.

3 Abd al-Rahman II (792–852)
Abderramán II founded the city of Mursiya (Murcia) in 825.

4 El Cid (1043–99)
This charismatic knight won considerable lands around Valencia from the Arabs.

5 Jaime I (1208–76)
The first to make major gains against the Arabs in the Costa Blanca.

6 Isabella I (1451–1504) and Ferdinand V (1452–1516)
The Catholic monarchs held court at Orihuela in 1488, with the city at its most influential.

7 Rodrigo de Borgia (1432–1503)
The infamous Pope Alexander VI, father of 10 children including Cesare and Lucrezia Borgia, was born in Xàtiva.

8 Barbarroja (1475–1546)
Turkish pirate Jayr al-Din – better known as Barbarroja ("Red Beard") – was the scourge of the Mediterranean.

9 José de Ribera (1591–1652)
One of Spain's finest painters, he was born in Xàtiva but spent most of his life in Italy.

10 José Moñino Redondo (1728–1808)
A key figure in the Spanish Enlightenment. Born in Murcia.

The spectacular Villena Treasure (see p54) *displays the highly sophisticated metalworking techniques of Bronze Age Spain.*

Left **Sierra de Espuña** Right **Isla Tabarca**

Top 10 Areas of Natural Beauty

1 Cap de la Nau (Cabo de la Nao)

This is the epitome of the Costa Blanca: a rugged cape with tiny, magical coves, many accessible only by boat, and sheer cliffs offering magnificent views along the whole coastline. While parts are covered with villas, there are still some beautiful undisturbed corners to explore. *Map H3*

2 Parc Natural del Montgó

The pale massif of Montgó looms high above the seaside resorts of Denia (Dénia) and Xàbia (Jávea). Delightful walking trails meander through flower-strewn scrub and woodland, past ancient caves and up to stunning view-points that gaze out across the sierra and over the sea. *Map H2*

3 Penyal d'Ifac (Peñón de Ifach), Calp (Calpe)

A vast, sheer rock erupting from the turquoise sea, the Penyal d'Ifac is a startling sight. Once a virtually impregnable pirate lair, it is now a Natural Park with a magnificent walking trail that will lead you right to the summit *(see pp16–17)*.

Penyal d'Ifac (Peñón de Ifach)

4 Fonts d'Algar

Tucked away in an orchard-lined valley, these enchanting waterfalls spill down the hillside and form a series of delightful natural swimming pools. A wooden staircase eases the ascent across boulders and rushing streams to the highest pool, which is shaded by willow trees and makes a perfect picnic spot *(see p73)*.

5 Parc Natural de la Font Roja

One of the few surviving stretches of indigenous Mediterranean oak forest, this glorious expanse of woodland is a cool, shady Natural Park scattered with ancient snow wells (used to collect ice in the days before refrigeration) and criss-crossed with beautiful walking trails offering spectacular views of endless mountains. *Map E3*

6 Isla de Benidorm

The natural beauty of this curious, triangular island in the middle of Benidorm Bay is best appreciated underwater, for the Isla de Benidorm is a marine reserve and home to a fabulous array of sea life, from sea anemones to octopus, stingray and scorpion fish. *Map G4*

7 Isla Tabarca

Tabarca, the only inhabited island on the Costa Blanca, has beautiful pebbly coves, a sandy bay, and a charming old town complete with a winsome little church right on the water's edge *(see pp24–5)*.

8 Sierra de Espuña

This magnificent range of pine-clad mountains is one of the few green corners of arid Murcia. Wonderful walking trails offer startling glimpses of forested slopes and rocky outcrops, and birds of prey wheel lazily, high above the treetops *(see pp20–21)*.

Fonts d'Algar

9 Calblanque

The Regional Park of Calblanque is one of Murcia's best-kept secrets. Just a few minutes' drive from the resorts of the Mar Menor, this stunning stretch of unspoilt coastline boasts hidden coves and gorgeous sandy beaches with perfectly clear waters *(see pp8–9)*.

10 Ciudad Encantada de Bolnuevo, Bolnuevo

The pale stone cliffs behind Bolnuevo Beach have been shaped over time into an extraordinary "enchanted city"; it doesn't take much to see towers and castles in the creamy swirls of rock, some of which are poised on impossibly thin pedestals *(see p94)*.

Top 10 Trees, Plants and Wildlife

1 Holm Oak

With its dark, waxy leaves this evergreen is common across the Iberian Peninsula.

2 Spanish Broom

This hardy evergreen is a beautiful sight in spring, when its glorious yellow blooms carpet the countryside.

3 Valencian Rock Violet

This pretty, purple, cliff-dwelling flower thrives in damp, salty conditions.

4 Fruit Trees

The orchards of the Costa Blanca produce almonds, citrus fruit and cherries.

5 Wild Herbs

Rosemary, thyme and lavender scent the scrubby slopes, particularly around the Montgó Natural Park.

6 Gulls

Many species of gull breed along the Costa Blanca, including the endangered Audouin's gull, with its trademark red bill and dark feet.

7 Birds of Prey

Eagles, hawks and vultures wheel silently above the more remote sierras of the northern Costa Blanca.

8 Flamingoes

During the summer, flamingoes come to breed on the salt lakes at Santa Pola, Torrevieja and the Mar Menor.

9 Ibex

This nimble mountain goat once faced extinction, but is now flourishing in the sierras of the northern Costa Blanca and parts of Murcia.

10 Wild Boar

These tusked, shaggy-coated mammals are common in most of the forested inland regions of the Costa Blanca.

Left **Denia** Right **Torrevieja**

Resorts

1 Denia (Dénia)
Dénia, now a relaxed family resort with great beaches and a busy port, had a long and glorious history before tourism hit the Mediterranean coast – first as a Roman settlement, then as the capital of an Arabic kingdom. For respite from the summer crowds, take a hike in the nearby Montgó Natural Park. *Map H2*

2 Xàbia (Jávea)
The pretty tumble of old Xàbia sits on a hilltop a couple of miles inland from the sea. The bay forms a perfect horseshoe, with a choice of pebbly or sandy beaches and a spectacular cape at both ends. *Map H3*

3 Calp (Calpe)
Calp has a stunning natural setting on a vast bay dominated by the Penyal d'Ifac *(see pp16–17, 36)*. The modern resort has almost swallowed up the original medieval village, but its sandy beaches and excellent water-sports facilities have made it immensely popular. *Map G3*

4 Altea
Pretty Altea, piled on a hill overlooking the sea and topped with a blue-domed church, has long attracted artists, and the old quarter is packed with arty shops and galleries. A narrow, pebbly beach is backed by an appealing seafront promenade, where the whole town comes to stroll on summer evenings. *Map G4*

5 Benidorm
The biggest and best-known of the Costa Blanca resorts, Benidorm is a mini-Manhattan of skyscrapers set around an impressive bay. Its immaculate beaches, two sweeping curves of golden sand, are the finest in the region, and the choice of restaurants and nightlife can't be beaten. *Map G4*

6 La Vila Joiosa (Villajoyosa)
The Jewelled Town gets its name from the brightly painted houses of ochre, yellow and blue which are clustered around the port. It has fine sandy beaches, a smattering of historic buildings, and a centuries-old chocolate-making tradition. *Map F4*

7 Torrevieja
Torrevieja is a low-key family resort with some great sandy beaches and an unusual but attractive seafront, with rock

Altea

La Vila Joiosa

pools accessed by ladders. The salt lagoons on the outskirts have been designated a Natural Park; you might well spot a cloud of pink flamingoes here. *Map Q3*

8 Santiago de la Ribera

A smart, upmarket resort on the shores of the Mar Menor, Santiago de la Ribera is popular with well-heeled Murcianos. The quiet waters of the inland sea make it the perfect place to learn to sail or windsurf, and the watersports facilities are excellent. *Map P4*

9 Puerto de Mazarrón

This sprawling family resort has several sandy beaches spread on either side of a rocky headland, which has an attractive coastal path. The inland village of Mazarrón is a tranquil spot for a break from the beach. *Map M5*

10 Águilas

Águilas is beautifully set on a curving bay against a backdrop of distant mountains. There are some handsome 19th-century squares, a dramatic castle high on a cliff above the fishing port, and dozens of secluded coves on the outskirts. Development has been largely low-key. *Map L6*

Top 10 Quiet Resorts

1 Oliva
Escape the crowds in this peaceful village, 4 km (2 miles) from lengthy golden beaches.

2 Moraira-Teulada
A smart enclave of whitewashed villas on a rugged coastline, with quiet coves and a marina.

3 El Campello
Despite the proximity of the busy beaches at San Juan, this fishing village retains its tranquil atmosphere.

4 Guardamar del Segura
This is a small, family resort blessed with wonderful, wild dune-backed beaches.

5 Dehesa de Campoamor
A modern resort of low-rise villas and apartments set around long, golden sands.

6 Lo Pagán
The smallest resort on the Mar Menor, Lo Pagán has great seafood restaurants on the beach.

7 Portús
This tiny village overlooks a narrow, sandy beach with colourful fishing boats. Its relative seclusion makes it popular with naturists.

8 Bolnuevo
On the fringes of Puerto de Mazarrón, Bolnuevo has long sandy beaches and hidden coves to the south.

9 La Azohía
On the unspoilt cape of Tiñoso, this fishing village is one of the quietest resorts in the region.

10 Calabardina
A charming little resort tucked under a dramatic headland and overlooking a delightful bay.

Left **The Calblanque coastline** Right **The beach at Benidorm**

TOP 10 Beaches

1 Playa de Venecia, Gandia-Playa

This immaculate golden beach is famously "combed" by tractors in summer to maintain its pristine appearance. Lined with smart rows of coconut-matting sunshades and blue-and-white-striped sun loungers, it has all the amenities: play areas for children, showers, lifeguard posts, and a line of restaurants and cafés along the seafront. ✎ *Map F1*

2 Les Aigües Blanques, Oliva

Oliva is blessed with long, sandy beaches that extend for miles so that you can always find a quiet spot if you are prepared to walk. This beach is the largest and best equipped, with every imaginable amenity. ✎ *Map G2*

3 Les Rotes, Denia (Dénia)

This is a delightful pebbly stretch of rock pools, tiny islands and hidden coves, where you can usually find a quiet corner. It has good amenities and a breezy seafront promenade lined with restaurants and cafés. ✎ *Map H2*

4 La Granadella, Cap de la Nau (Cabo de la Nao)

The only way in and out of this tiny, pebbly cove is a narrow road which twists and turns down to the perfect curve of the bay. The blue-green water is overlooked by cliffs, and the small rocky beach is backed by just a couple of café-bars. ✎ *Map H3*

La Granadella

5 Portitxol, Cap de la Nau

This is another exquisite cove, flanked by high cliffs and looking out over the tiny island of Portitxol. The viewing point *(mirador)* above the cove offers some of the most beautiful views on the whole coastline. Amenities include a handful of café-bars and a lifeguard post. ✎ *Map H3*

6 Playa de Poniente and Playa de Levante, Benidorm

The golden arc of Benidorm's twin beaches stretches for almost five km (3 miles) around the bay, a breathtaking sweep of gleaming sand and turquoise waters. In high season, you'll need to get there early to grab some space. Immaculate and superbly equipped with everything from play areas and wheelchair ramps to beach bars and lifeguard posts. ✎ *Map F4, G4*

Tourist offices have a useful brochure listing all the beaches and their facilities.

7 Playa de San Juan, Alicante (Alacant)

Easily the best of Alicante's beaches, this glorious stretch of fine sand with every facility is in a popular holiday suburb a short tram ride from the city centre. The bars and clubs buzz all night in summer. Ⓝ *Map E5*

8 Dunas de Guardamar, Guardamar del Segura

These gorgeous, windswept dunes are rarely crowded, even in the height of summer. They are part of a natural reserve backed by a pine forest with walking trails, interesting archaeological remains and picnic spots. There are a few snack bars, but little else. Ⓝ *Map Q2*

9 Calblanque

Calblanque *(see pp8–9)* is one of the most beautiful stretches of coastline on the Costa Blanca, with golden beaches, secluded coves, cliff walks and forested hills. It has few facilities, so bring picnic things and plenty of water. Take care: the current can be dangerous. Ⓝ *Map P5*

10 Playa de Bolnuevo, Bolnuevo

The main beach of this sleepy little resort is long and sandy, with good facilities including lifeguards, cafés and restaurants. Behind it are the extraordinary cliffs of the "Enchanted City" *(see p94)*. To the south, naturists will find a series of secluded coves. Ⓝ *Map M5*

Playa de Bolnuevo

Top 10 Beach Survival Tips

1 Blue Flags
Blue Flags are awarded to beaches which have achieved a high standard of cleanliness and offer good facilities.

2 Warning Flags
Don't swim if a red flag is flying, and be cautious if you see a yellow flag. A green flag means it is safe to swim.

3 Facilities
Town beaches generally offer excellent facilities, including play areas, foot showers and refreshments.

4 Jellyfish
Jellyfish can be a nuisance. If you get stung, larger beaches will have a medical post.

5 Lifeguards
Most beaches, even more remote ones, will have a lifeguard post in summer.

6 Sunscreen
Don't forget your sunscreen! The sun is very fierce on the Costa Blanca. You should avoid sunbathing between noon and 4pm.

7 Water
Ensure you bring an adequate water supply, particularly when staying on remote beaches.

8 Beach bars
Many beaches have snack bars, or *xiringuitos*, which open only in the summer.

9 Beating the crowds
The Costa Blanca is highly developed, and city beaches are always crammed, but you can always find a quiet corner.

10 Wheelchair Access
Many beaches, particularly those in the cities, have special ramps for wheelchair access. The tourist office will have details.

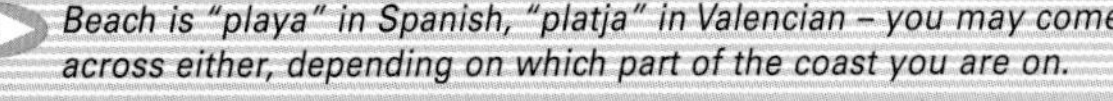

Beach is "playa" in Spanish, "platja" in Valencian – you may come across either, depending on which part of the coast you are on.

Left **Vall del Segura** Right **Denia to Granadella: view from the coast road**

Top 10 Walks and Drives

Planes (Vall de Gallinera drive)

1 Vall de Gallinera (Drive)

If you can, visit the Vall de Gallinera in spring, when the scent of almond blossom fills the air, and the hillsides are covered with a sea of pink and white. The CV–700 from Pego to Planes is a scenic mountain road, winding past medieval villages, ghostly Arabic settlements, lush orchards and ruined castles. To extend the drive, head for the lovely village of Agres *(see p46)*. *Map G2–F3*

2 Vall del Segura (Drive)

This drive follows the Segura River from the cosmopolitan city of Murcia to the country town of Calasparra *(see p104)*. Along the way, take time out at Archena's pretty spa (good for lunch and a dip in the pool), then meander through the green valley of Ricote up to historic Cieza, past the lake of Alfonso XIII, which attracts many birds, finishing up among the rice fields of Calasparra. *Map N3–K1*

3 Montgó (Hike)

The hike to the top of Montgó begins at the entrance to the park and climbs steadily, past ancient caves and scrubby hills covered with wild herbs and flowers, up to the Creueta at 753 m (2,470 ft). The hike is easy, but it takes about three hours each way – well worth it, though, since a tremendous view of the dramatic coastline unfolds. *Map H2*

4 Vall de Guadalest (Drive)

From the seaside resort of Altea to the hilltop village of Penáguila, this drive takes in waterfalls and natural pools near Callosa d'en Sarrià (Fonts d'Algar, *see pp36, 73*), the precipitous village of Guadalest overlooking a turquoise lake *(see pp14–15)*, and, approached through olive groves and rugged passes, the serene, castle-topped village of Penáguila. *Map G4–E3*

Vall de Guadalest

5 Racó del Duc (Walk)

An abandoned railway line has been converted into an excellent walking and cycling path which follows the River Serpis over bridges and through tunnels, past gorges, waterfalls, ruined castles and woodland glades, from Villalonga to L'Orxa. It's an easy trail which takes about three to four hours to walk. Bring a picnic and a swimming costume. ✆ *Map F2*

6 Sierra de Bernia (Hike)

There are several hikes from the Fonts d'Algar; a short walk from the falls will bring you to the substantial ruins of the Fortress of Bernia, where experienced walkers can continue on to the demanding circuit around the peak itself. The hike requires some simple climbing moves and takes about seven hours. ✆ *Map G3*

Sierra Espuña

7 Sierra de Espuña (Hikes)

The Sierra de Espuña is probably the best place for walking in the area, with a range of trails adapted to hikers of all abilities. There are short trails for families, and more demanding hikes for advanced walkers *(see pp20–21)*. ✆ *Map L3*

8 Parc Natural de la Font Roja (Walk)

The sanctuary at the heart of the Parc Natural de la Font Roja is a popular weekend day trip for locals. The shady walking paths through Mediterranean oak forest are the perfect respite from searing summer heat. There are walking trails to suit hikers of all levels, with the easiest (suitable for families) leaving from the sanctuary itself. ✆ *Map E3*

9 Wine country: Monóvar, Jumilla, Yecla (Drive)

Take a tour of the *bodegas* in the delightful wine towns of Monóvar, Jumilla and Yecla *(see p56)*. Lost in a sea of vines, this drive is at its best in the late summer or early autumn just before harvest. Begin at sleepy Monóvar and finish in Yecla, the largest and prettiest of the three. ✆ *Map C5–B4*

10 Coast Road, Denia (Dénia) to Granadella (Drive)

This scenic coastal drive twists over scrubby hills past the Natural Park of Montgó, through the whitewashed village of Xàbia (Jávea), around the dramatic headland of the Cap de la Nau (Cabo de la Nao), to the tiny cove of Granadella. It's one to avoid in high summer, though. ✆ *Map H2–3*

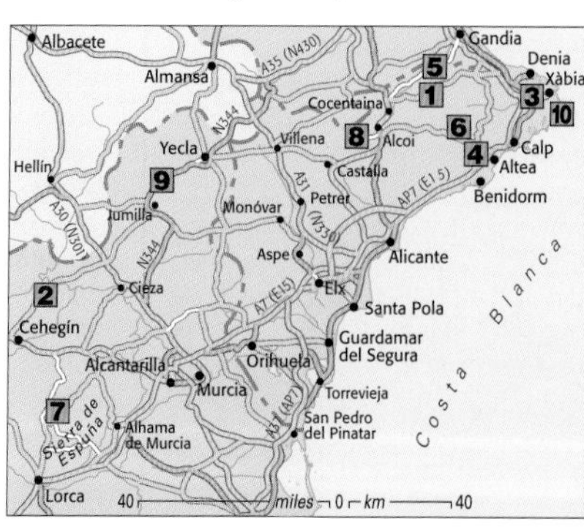

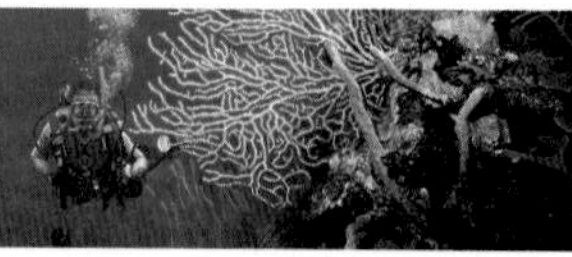

Left **Sailing on the Mar Menor** Right **Diving off Cabo de Palos**

Outdoor Activities and Sports

1 Snorkelling and Diving

The Costa Blanca offers endless possiblities for underwater exploration, and several areas have been declared marine reserves, including the Cap de Sant Antoni near Xàbia (Jávea), the Isla de Benidorm, the Penyal d'Ifac *(see pp16–17)* and the Isla Tabarca *(see p24–5)*. There are companies offering diving courses and trips in all the major resorts.

2 Adventure Sports

The mountainous inland regions are fantastic for adventure sports. You can try your hand at canyon-descent, bungee-jumping, canoeing, rafting, hang-gliding, quad-biking or off-roading.

3 Hiking and Rock-climbing

The coastal cliffs and inland sierras are perfect for hiking and climbing. The Penyal d'Ifac and the Sierra de Bernia have several challenging climbing routes, and the Natural Parks, particularly the Sierra de Espuña *(see pp20–21)*, Font Roja *(see p36)*, Montgó *(see p36)* and Calblanque *(see pp8–9)*, offer dozens of great hikes and walking trails.

Cycling in the Calblanque Natural Park

Golf course at La Manga Club

4 Cycling

Cycling is a very popular sport in Spain. Some resorts have bike-rental facilities if you simply want to cruise the region on two wheels, and the Natural Parks have several off-road trails for mountain-bikers.

5 Golf

With its year-round sunshine and mild temperatures, it's hardly surprising that the Costa Blanca is one of the top golfing destinations in Europe. There are scores of courses, of which the best known is probably the luxurious La Manga Club, with three championship courses. *La Manga Club: www.lamangaclub.com*

6 Sailing

Most resorts have a marina offering everything from sailing courses to yacht charter and skipper hire. The biggest marinas are in Calp (Calpe), Benidorm, Alicante (Alacant), Torrevieja and Santiago de la Ribera.

7 Bird-watching
The Costa Blanca region is a veritable paradise for bird-watching enthusiasts. The salt lagoons in Calp, Santa Pola, Torrevieja and Calblanque attract numerous aquatic birds, and the sierras, particularly the Regional Park of the Sierra Espuña, are home to eagles and other birds of prey.

8 Fishing
Fishing is a long-standing obsession in Spain, but be aware that permits are often required for both freshwater and deep-sea fishing. Contact the tourist information offices for further details. Taking an organized fishing holiday can sidestep the need for a permit, because the tour company will arrange these for you.

Windsurfing

9 Other Watersports
Windsurfing, surfing, water-skiing and jet-skiing are popular sports along the Costa Blanca. You'll find facilities for all of these in all the larger seaside resorts.

10 Horse riding
There are horse-riding centres across the region, and most can organize anything from pony rides for kids to cross-country hacks. Tourist information offices have lists of local riding centres.

Top 10 Spanish Sports Stars

1 Fernando Alonso
This 2005 and 2006 Formula One Grand Prix champion is the youngest person ever to win the title.

2 Severiano Ballesteros
Perhaps the most famous golfer that Spain has ever produced, Ballesteros has now retired.

3 Sergio García
This sensational young golfer has caused a storm since his first appearance on the international circuit.

4 Iker Casillas
This Real Madrid goal-keeper is one of the key players of the Spanish national team.

5 Carlos Moyá
One of Spain's greatest tennis champions, and winner of numerous titles.

6 Miguel Indurain
Champion cyclist, and five-time consecutive winner of the Tour de France.

7 Arantxa Sánchez Vicario
Spain's finest female tennis champion has won several Grand Slam tournaments.

8 Carlos Sainz
Carlos Sainz is twice World Rally champion (1990 and 1992). He holds a record 26 World Rally wins and 97 podium finishes.

9 Rafael Nadal
Currently one of the world's top-ranking tennis stars.

10 Pau Gasol
Basketball is incredibly popular in Spain, and this player, one of the best around, plays for the Los Angeles Lakers in the American National Basketball Association.

Caravaca de la Cruz

TOP 10 Medieval Villages

1 Agres

This delightful mountain village topped by a ruined castle makes the perfect starting point for exploring the gorgeous Sierra Mariola, with hiking trails and the traces of abandoned snow wells. *Map E3*

2 Cocentaina

The ancient core of Cocentaina is a charming tangle of crooked streets set around the imposing Palau Condal. The palace marks the dividing point between the Christian and Arab quarters which were established after the Reconquest. A ruined Arabic watchtower still stands guard on a lofty cliff. *Map E3*

3 Bocairent

Unexpected steps and tiny passages link the steep streets of Bocairent, piled up on a hill in the Sierra Mariola. Almost every house is surrounded by pots of ferns and geraniums. In 1843, an extraordinary bullring was hacked out of the rock. It now regularly hosts summer concerts. *Map D3*

Guadalest town square

4 Guadalest

The most famous inland village in the Costa Blanca, Guadalest has a picture-postcard setting atop a jagged crest in a sea of mountains *(see pp14–15)*.

5 Penáguila

Time seems to have stood still in Penáguila, a small village of ochre houses huddled around a sturdy 16th-century church. On the outskirts are the immaculate flower gardens and ponds of the 19th-century Jardín de Santos. Surrounded by magnificent mountains, the ruins of an ancient castle are set among forest high above the village. *Map F3*

6 Polop

Just a few miles inland from the hectic coast, Polop is a peaceful little village on a hill surrounded by orchards. Often overlooked in the rush to the beaches, Polop's old quarter, with its maze of narrow streets recalling its Arabic origins, invites a tranquil stroll. *Map G4*

7 Caravaca de la Cruz

Beautifully set in rolling hills, this medieval town *(see p103)* resonates with history. It belonged to the Knights Templar after the Reconquest, and is dominated by the 15th-century castle. Within the castle complex is the unmissable Santuario de la Vera Cruz, which houses what is believed to be a fragment of the Cross. *Map K2*

Mula

8 Steeply mounted on a sheer cliff, Mula (see p104) is guarded by an imposing castle. Narrow streets meander between handsome squares lined with 16th-century churches and palaces. On the outskirts, there's a fine spa, in use since Roman times. ⓢ *Map L2*

Polop village

Moratalla

9 Sleepy Moratalla lies on a hillside in the remotest corner of Murcia, a jumble of tiled rooftops under a castle built by the Arabs and then rebuilt after the Reconquest. The streets are so steep that the locals get around on mopeds. A viewing point near the castle offers fine views. ⓢ *Map K1*

Cehegín

10 Cehegín perches gracefully on a hillside overlooking the river. Its elegant, well-preserved old quarter, with a swathe of medieval churches and mansions bearing coats of arms, still displays vestiges of its aristocratic past. The best views of the surrounding country are from a balustraded viewing point at the top. ⓢ *Map K2*

Top 10 Castles

1 Biar

This well-preserved Arabic castle withstood a lengthy siege before finally falling to Jaime I (see pp34–5) in 1245. ⓢ *Map D4*

2 Villena

High above the town, this fairytale castle has crenellated towers and sturdy ramparts (see p73). ⓢ *Map C4*

3 Petrer (Petrel)

Precipitously balanced on a razor-thin cliff, this castle was built by the Arabs (see p85). ⓢ *Map D4*

4 Xàtiva (Játiva)

The Romans built a fortress here, but the current castle dates back to the medieval period. ⓢ *Map E1*

5 Banyeres de Mariola

The highest castle in the region, it dominates a lofty peak. ⓢ *Map D3*

6 Guadalest

Little is left of Guadalest's castle, but the ruins offer panoramic views (see pp14–15).

7 Castillo de Santa Bárbara, Alicante (Alacant)

This imposing 16th-century fortress replaced the original Arabic castle (see pp10–11).

8 La Mola

This curious castle, with the only triangular tower in Europe, is next to a Modernista sanctuary. ⓢ *Map D5*

9 Denia (Dénia)

The design of Denia's castle dates back to the Muslim period (see p34). ⓢ *Map H2*

10 Águilas

Beautifully flood-lit at night, this cliff-top castle is perched right on the cliff edge. ⓢ *Map L6*

Left **Casa de El Piñón, La Unión** Right **Ceiling detail, Torrevieja Casino**

TOP 10 Modernista Gems

1 Casa-Museo Modernista, Novelda

The most sumptuous Modernista mansion in the Costa Blanca has been exquisitely restored, and still contains much of its original furniture *(see pp18–19).*

Casa-Museo Modernista, Novelda

2 Círculo Industrial, Alcoi (Alcoy)

Alcoi, still a busy industrial town, has several Modernista buildings. The Círculo Industrial (1868) was one of the earliest. Particularly worthy of note are the flowing ironwork and ceramic details in its fine salons and library. Designed as a cultural centre, it still hosts art exhibitions and the occasional concert. It also has a restaurant. *C/San Nicolas 19 • Map E3 • 965 54 06 66 • Open 9am–9pm daily • Free*

3 Casa Familia Monerris Planelles, Xixona (Jijona)

Xixona is most famous for its production of sweet nougat *(turrón)*, but it also contains some handsome turn-of-the-20th-century buildings. This mansion, belonging to a family of *turroneros*, sports a lovely façade, thickly covered with brilliant blue and gold tiles and painted griffons. *Avda de la Constitución 33–35–37 • Map E4*

4 Casino, Torrevieja

Torrevieja's celebrated seafront casino is one of the purest examples of Modernista architecture in the region. The highlight is the Mozarabic salon, with a fabulous carved wooden ceiling, horseshoe arches and shimmering mosaic tiling. *Paseo Vistalegre 14 • Map Q3 • 965 71 01 04 • Visits by appointment • Free*

5 Casa Modernista, Jumilla

This architectural gem of the early 20th century is tucked away in the quiet wine-producing town of Jumilla. Designed by a follower of Gaudí, it boasts impressive, highly ornate ironwork by local craftsman Avelino Gómez. *C/Canovas del Castillo 55 • Map A4 • Closed to public*

6 Casino, Murcia

Currently closed for renovation, Murcia's breathtaking casino *(see p30)* is a monument to eclecticism. Each room has a different theme, from the Arabic-style entrance hall with a ceiling that drips like icing, to the flamboyant Rococo frills and flounces in the ballroom. And there's a special bonus for female visitors: the mural of primping nymphs in the ladies' restroom.

Library in the Círculo Industrial, Alcoi

7 Palacio de Aguirre, Cartagena

The most prolific Modernista architect in Cartagena at the turn of the 20th century was Victor Beltrí, who was responsible for this beautiful mansion in the heart of the old town. Profusely decorated with shimmering tiled mosaics and topped with a brilliant cupola, its corner position was chosen to ensure plenty of natural light. ⊗ *Plaza de la Merced 16 • Map P5 • Info from Cartagena tourist office: 968 50 64 83 • Open for occasional exhibitions*

8 Casino, Cartagena

This 18th-century Baroque palace was completely overhauled at the end of the 19th century, when the property was taken over by the Casino Círculo Cartagenero, a social and cultural club. Victor Beltrí was responsible for adding the ornate Modernista woodwork, floral tiling and exuberant plasterwork, which are now sadly neglected. ⊗ *C/Mayor 15 • Map P5 • 968 52 55 77 • Open 10am–1:30pm, 5–9:30pm daily • Free*

9 Gran Hotel, Cartagena

Crowned with its trademark golden cupola, the most emblematic Modernista building in the whole of Cartagena, the opulent Gran Hotel, was begun in 1907 by Tomás Rico and completed by the indefatigable Victor Beltrí. Every window and archway is surrounded with swooping stone garlands. It is no longer a hotel, and visitors must be content with admiring its exterior. ⊗ *C/Jara s/n • Map P5 • Info from Cartagena tourist office: 968 50 64 83 • Closed to public*

10 Casa de El Piñón, La Unión

The Casa de El Piñón is one of the best examples of Murcian eclecticism, bristling with florid decoration and topped with a cupola which was designed by Gustave Eiffel. The building has finally been restored after years of neglect, and now houses local government offices. ⊗ *C/Mayor s/n • Map P5 • Info from La Unión tourist office: 968 541 614 • Closed to public*

Moors and Christians

Top 10 Festivals and Events

1 Semana Santa (Holy Week)

Every town and village has parades and processions during Holy Week, but the Murcia region in particular is renowned for its spectacular celebrations. The Holy Week processions in Lorca, Murcia City, Cartagena, Mula and Moratalla are all justifiably famous, but those in Alicante (Alacant) and Orihuela are also well worth seeing *(see p31)*.

Semana Santa procession

2 Moros y Cristianos (Moors and Christians)

Mock battles between Moors and Christians have been held for centuries. The most famous one is held in Alcoi (Alcoy) around 24 April, but most villages have their own version.

3 Las Hogueras de San Juan (Bonfires of Saint John)

The Feast of St John the Baptist on 24 June is celebrated in the Costa Blanca with bonfires, fireworks and parades. Alicante's festival is the biggest *(see p13)*.

4 Fira de Tots Sants (All Saints Fair)

Cocentaina has celebrated All Saints on 1 November every year since 1346; it's one of the oldest traditional fairs in Spain. Originally an agricultural and grain market, it is now a hugely popular medieval-style fair selling all kinds of local produce from honey to cheese.

5 Misteri d'Elx (Elche) (Mystery of Elx)

The origins of this medieval mystery play – the only one to have survived a 17th-century ban by the Council of Trent – date back to the 13th century. It is performed in mid-August every year and at the start of November every even year in the Basílica de Santa María in Elx *(see p83)*.

6 Bous a la Mar (Bulls in the Sea)

The culmination of Denia's summer festival in the first fortnight of August is the Bous a la Mar, when bulls are sent careering down the streets, chased by the bravest locals; it's the locals, rather than the bulls, who end up in the sea!

7 Carnavales (Carnival)

Carnival, usually held in February, gives everyone a chance to let off steam before Lent, and there are wild parties across the region. The village of Pego in the northern Costa Blanca puts on a good show, but the best of all is in Águilas.

8 Fiesta de los Caballos del Vino (Festival of the Knights of Wine)

According to a medieval legend, the Knights Templar broke out of the besieged castle in Caravaca de la Cruz on a desperate search for water, but all they could find was wine. The story is recalled on 2 May each year, when richly dressed horses and horsemen process from the castle, and the local wine is blessed.

Festival of the Knights of Wine

9 Festival de Las Habaneras (Festival of Habaneras)

Habaneras are plaintive sea shanties, which get their name from the Cuban city where many Spaniards went to seek their fortunes – Havana. Torrevieja hosts an excellent festival in mid-August, when choral groups present contemporary and traditional songs.

10 Mar de Músicas

Held every July in Cartagena, this world music festival has become one of the best of its kind in Europe. Concerts are held in the town hall square, the ancient cathedral, and other beautiful settings around the old quarter. ✆ *www.lamardemusicas.com*

Top 10 Pilgrimages

1 Ermita de la Santa Eulalia, near Aledo

A popular pilgrimage to this mountain sanctuary. ✆ *Map L4 • 7 Jan*

2 Santuario de la Esperanza, Calasparra

Pilgrimage in honour of a miraculous image of the Virgin. ✆ *Map K1 • 7 Sep*

3 Romería de la Virgen, San Pedro del Pinatar

The image of the Virgin is taken by boat around the Mar Menor. ✆ *Map P3 • 16 Jul*

4 Romería de la Virgen de la Salud, Archena

A pilgrimage in honour of the town's patron saint. ✆ *Map M2 • Late May/early Jun*

5 Santuario del Monte de la Atalaya, Cieza

A procession from Cieza to the mountain sanctuary of the Virgen del Buen Suceso. ✆ *Map M1 • 3rd Sun in Sep*

6 Santuario de Nuestra Señora de la Fuensanta, Murcia

Pilgrimage to honour Murcia's patron saint. ✆ *Map N3 • Sep*

7 Santuario de la Mare de Déu del Castell, Agres

Pilgrimage in honour of a miraculous appearance of the Virgin. ✆ *Map E3 • Sep*

8 Monasterio de la Santa Faz, Alicante

Popular pilgrimage to this monastery *(see p12)*. ✆ *Map E5 • 2nd Thu after Easter Sun*

9 Santuario de la Virgen de los Lirios, nr Alcoi

In honour of Alcoi's patron saint. ✆ *Map E3 • 3rd Sun in Sep*

10 Santuario de la Virgen de las Virtudes, Villena

A pilgrimage in honour of Villena's patron saint. ✆ *Map C4 • Last Sun in Aug*

Left **Colegio de Santo Domingo, Orihuela** Right **Ex-Colegiata de San Patricio, Lorca**

TOP 10 Churches and Monasteries

1 Catedral de Santa María, Murcia

Murcia's impressive cathedral is best known for its flamboyant, sculpture-encrusted façade and florid bell tower *(see pp28–9)*.

2 Colegio de Santo Domingo, Orihuela

Often dubbed the "El Escorial of the East" after the celebrated royal palace near Madrid, this enormous complex was built between the 16th and 18th centuries. *C/Adolfo Claravana 63 • Map P2 • Open 10am–2pm, 4–7pm Tue–Sat (10am–2pm, 5–8pm in summer), 10am–2pm Sun • Free*

3 Santa Iglesia Catedral del Salvador, Orihuela

Orihuela's Gothic cathedral of pale, creamy stone was begun in the 14th century. There is exquisite sculptural detail inside and out. Two splendid wrought-iron grills enclose the choir, with its beautiful Baroque organ, and the main altar. *Plaza del Salvador • Map P2 • Open 10am–2pm, 4–7pm Mon–Fri, 10am–2pm & during Mass Sat, Sun • Free*

4 Ex-Colegiata de San Patricio, Lorca

This church commemorates victories against the Arabs on the feast day of San Patricio in 1452. Begun in the mid-16th century, it was given a thorough Baroque overhaul in the 18th. *Plaza España • Map K4 • 968 44 19 14 (tourist office) • Open 11am–1pm, 4:30–6:30pm daily (to 8pm Sat, Sun) & during Mass • Free*

Concatedral de San Nicolás de Bari, Alicante

5 Basílica de Santa María, Elx (Elche)

Celebrated for its performances of the Misteri d'Elx *(see p50)*, the monumental Basílica de Santa María was built between 1672 and 1783, replacing an earlier church built on the ruins of a former mosque. *Plaza de Santa María • Map D6, Q1 • Info: 965 45 15 40 • Open 7am–1:30pm, 5:30–9pm daily • Free (except for the tower)*

6 Concatedral de San Nicolás de Bari, Alicante (Alacant)

Dedicated to the city's patron saint, Alicante's vast cathedral *(see p12)* was built in the sober Herreran style. Its most striking feature is the graceful blue cupola almost 50 m (164 ft) high.

7 Basílica de Santa María, Alicante

This delightful church was built on the ruins of Al-Lekant's main mosque before the Reconquest. The soaring interior is in the purest Gothic style. The frothy façade was added in 1713 *(see p12)*.

8 Iglesia de San Bartolomé, Xàbia (Jávea)

The fortress-church of San Bartolomé was begun in 1513, when the coastline was under constant attack from pirates, but the golden Tosca stone and its faded sculptural decoration make it truly charming. *Plaza de la Iglesia • Map H3 • 965 79 11 74 • Open 11am–1pm, 5:30–7:30pm Mon–Wed, Fri–Sun • Free*

9 Colegiata Basílica de Santa María, Xàtiva (Játiva)

The grandest church in this "City of Popes" was begun in 1596, but remains unfinished. The façade was finally constructed in 1916; the second bell tower (proposed 300 years ago) has yet to be built. *Plaza Calixto III • Map E1 • 962 27 33 46 (tourist office) • Open 10:30am–1pm daily (to 11am Mon) • Free*

10 Iglesia de San Martìn, Callosa de Segura

Once one of the most affluent cities of the old Kingdom of Valencia, Callosa de Segura possesses one of the finest Renaissance churches in Spain. *Plaza de la Iglesia • Map P2 • 966 75 70 59 (call to arrange a visit) • Free*

Iglesia de San Bartolomé, Xàbia

Top 10 Architectural Styles and Terms

1 Romanesque (c.1050–c.1200)
Inspired by Roman architecture; characterized by rounded arches and tunnel vaults.

2 Gothic (c.1250–1550)
Typical features: elaborate masonry and woodwork, pointed arches and exterior flying buttresses.

3 Renaissance (c.1450–1600)
Renaissance architects took inspiration from monuments of Greco-Roman civilization.

4 Baroque (c.1600–1750)
Spanish Baroque features undulating façades with high relief and ornate decoration.

5 Modernista (c.1880–c.1920)
A regional variation on Art Nouveau: flowing lines, organic forms, and highly detailed decorative elements.

6 Múdejar
A fusion of Christian and Islamic art created by the Arabs who remained in Spain after the Reconquest.

7 Artesonado
Elaborately carved marquetry ceilings introduced by the Arabs, but absorbed into the Christian tradition after the Reconquest.

8 Azulejos
Elaborate tiles, many produced in the Costa Blanca region using techniques introduced by the Arabs.

9 Churrigueresque
The Baroque style at its most ornate and overblown.

10 Retablo Mayor
An altarpiece, usually featuring a series of painted panels, decorates the main altar in most Spanish churches.

Left **MARQ** Right **MUBAG**

TOP 10 Museums

1 MARQ, Alicante (Alacant)

This slickly designed new museum *(see p12)* brings Alicante's past to life. As well as sections devoted to each phase of history, there are fascinating recreations of archeological sites, including a wreck containing amphorae.

Tesoro de Villena

2 MAHE, Elx (Elche)

Situated in the Palacio de Altamira, this museum was inaugurated in 2006, and displays a fine range of archaeological remains, which explain the history of Elx from its origins to the present day. *Palau d'Altamira, Carrer Nou del Palau • Map D6 • 966 65 82 03 • Open 10am–1:30pm, 4:30–8pm Tue–Sat, 10:30am–1:30pm Sun • Adm charge*

3 MUBAG, Alicante

A beautifully restored 18th-century palace houses this wide-ranging collection of paintings, furniture, ceramics and engravings by Alicantino artists. Concerts are frequently held here too, check the website for details. *Palacio Conde Lumiares, C/Gravina 13–15 • Map V2 • 965 14 67 80 • Open 10am–2pm, 4–8pm Tue–Sat (May–Sep: 5–9pm), 10am–2pm Sun • www.mubag.org • Free*

4 Museo Arqueológico, Villena

The prize exhibit here is the Villena Treasure (Tesoro de Villena) – a glittering Bronze Age hoard of bracelets, bowls, torcs and bottles, fashioned from thin sheets of beaten gold, and skilfully decorated with simple incisions or raised patterns. *Palacio Municipal, Plaza de Santiago 1 • Map C4 • 965 80 11 50 (ext 766) • www.museovillena.com • Open 10am–2pm, 5–8pm Tue–Fri, 11am–2pm Sat • Free*

5 Museo del Calzado, Elda

This intriguing museum in Spain's shoe-making capital documents the evolution of shoe design from the early spurred metal boots worn by medieval knights to the most extravagant 21st-century creations. If you love shoes, don't miss it. *Avda de Chapí 32 • Map D4 • 965 38 30 21 • Open Sep–Jul: 10am–1pm, 4–8pm Tue–Sat, 11am–2pm Sun; Aug: 11am–2pm Sun • www.museocalzado.com • Adm charge*

Portrait of Felipe V, Museo de l'Almudí

6 Museo San Juan de Dios, Orihuela

The 18th-century Hospital of San Juan de Dios is the graceful home of Orihuela's archaeological museum, which recounts the history of the city from its earliest beginnings to the 18th century. The eeriest exhibit is a 17th-century processional float depicting a she-devil known as *La Diablesa*. ✆ *C/Hospital • Map P2 • 966 74 31 54 • Open 10am–2pm, 5–8pm Tue-Sat, 10am–2pm Sun • Free*

7 Museo de l'Almudí, Xàtiva (Játiva)

This much-restored 16th-century granary is home to fragments of Iberian sculpture and Visigothic capitals, as well as a large collection of paintings, including several works by Xàtiva-born José de Ribera. A portrait of King Felipe V is famously hung the wrong way up, as punishment for his burning the city down in 1707. ✆ *C/Corretgeria 46 • Map E1 • 962 27 65 97 • Open summer: 9:30am–2:30pm Tue-Fri, 10am–2pm Sat-Sun; winter 10am–2pm, 4–6pm Tue-Fri, 10am–2pm Sat-Sun • Adm charge*

La Diablesa

8 Museu Valencià del Joguet, Ibi

Kids of all ages will enjoy this museum, which has everything from puppets to train sets, miniature tea services and model aeroplanes. The exhibits date mainly from the early 20th century, and come from all parts of the world. ✆ *Plaza de la Iglesia • Map E4 • 966 55 02 26 • Open 10am–1pm, 4–7pm Tue-Sat, 11am–2pm Sun & public hols • www.museojuguete.com • Adm charge (free Sun & public hols)*

9 Museo Salzillo, Murcia

Dedicated to the 18th-century Murcian sculptor Francisco Salzillo *(see pp30–31)*, this museum contains a collection of gilded processional floats bearing his exquisite, highly emotional depictions of the Passion of Christ. Adjoining galleries display a large number of nativity figures *(belenes)*.

10 Museo del Teatro Romano, Cartagena

Discovered in 1988 and beautifully restored, the Roman theatre in Cartagena dates back to the first century BC. Visitors to this fascinating museum walk through a vast collection of archaeological remains before reaching the climax of the visit – the theatre itself. ✆ *C/Cuesta de la Baronesa • Map P5 • Open 10am–8pm Tue-Sat, 10am–2pm Sun • Adm charge*

Left **Bullas** Right **Hondón**

Top 10 Wine Towns

1 Jumilla

One of the largest wine-producing towns in Murcia, Jumilla spills down a hillside, overlooked by a 15th-century castle *(see p103)*. The town has been producing wine since Roman times. The local *bodegas* make a robust red from monastrell and a rosé from garnacha grapes. *Map A4*

Jumilla Castle

2 Yecla

Yecla is the prettiest of all the wine towns in the Costa Blanca, with a smattering of historic churches and buildings. It's best known for its red wines, which are generally light and fruity. Many *bodegas* offer tastings and tours. *Map B4*

3 Bullas

This medieval village, still guarded by the remnants of a battered castle, sits in a lush valley with endless snaking rows of vines. Wine has been produced here since Roman times; you can learn about its history at the local Museo del Vino. Good for rosés and red table wines. *Map L2*

4 Abanilla

Abanilla is a small, sunny agricultural town known for its palm groves. Although tucked just inside the boundary of Murcia province, it produces much of its wine under the Alicante D.O. – robust reds and some whites, usually drunk young and ideally suited to the earthy local cuisine. *Map N1*

5 Monóvar

A cheerful old town dotted with historic monuments, Monóvar is one of the biggest wine-producing towns in the Alicante region. At the many *bodegas* you can pick up some potent local red, a fresh rosé, or the celebrated El Fondillón, a sweet dessert wine which takes 20 years to mature. *Map D5*

6 Alguenya (Algueña)

This small agricultural village is well known for its hearty traditional cuisine, particularly cured sausages. The local wine, a strong, earthy red produced under the D.O. of Alicante, is perfect with regional dishes. *Map C5*

7 Hondón

Blink and you'll miss these two tiny hamlets in the middle of a vast plain with vines stretching in every direction. Hondón de las Nieves and Hondón de los Frailes are just off the Monóvar–Jumilla road. Their table wines are available from the large *bodegas* which line the road. *Map C5*

Jumilla, Yecla and Bullas have been granted their own D.O. (Denominación de Origen), *which guarantees quality.*

8 **El Pinós (Pinoso)**
Sitting peacefully on a low hill in a broad, vine-covered plain, El Pinós is an affluent little town with a rambling old centre curling around a pretty clock tower. It made its fortune from salt and cured sausages, but it is also an important wine-producing town. Try the vigorous young reds at one of many *bodegas*. *Map E5*

9 **Teulada**
The smart, upmarket resort of Teulada has long been famous for its moscatel grapes, grown along the sunny hillsides and sold in markets and at roadside stalls. They are used to make its delicious and refreshing sweet white *mistela* wine, which you will find at countless local *bodegas*. *Map H3*

10 **Xaló (Jalón)**
Dominated by its striking 19th-century church, the formerly sleepy village of Xaló is now surrounded by endless villas and holiday home developments. These days, tourism is its biggest source of income, but some traditions, including wine-production, have continued. There are several *bodegas*, with reds, whites, rosés and a sweet white *mistela* wine. *Map G3*

The vineyards of Monóvar

Top 10 Bodegas

1 **Bodegas Balcona**
Try the red Vino de Autor 2002. *Ctra Avilés Km 10, Paraje de Aceniche • Map K2 • 968 65 28 91*

2 **Bodegas Agapito Rico**
Excellent reds under the Carchelo label. *Casa de la Hoya s/n, Paraje El Carche, Jumilla • Map A4 • 968 43 55 09*

3 **Bodegas Bleda**
Try the award-winning Castillo de Jumilla Crianza 2005. *Paraje Omblancas, Jumilla • Map A4 • 968 78 00 12*

4 **Bodegas Gutiérrez de la Vega**
Don't forget to try the Costa Diva. *C/Canalejas 4, Parcent • Map G3 • 966 40 52 66*

5 **Bodegas E Mendoza**
Taste the excellent Reserva Santa Rosa. *Partida El Romeral s/n, L'Alfas del Pi • Map G4 • 965 88 86 39*

6 **Bodegas Castaño**
Very reputable, with good, fruity reds. *Ctra Fuenteálamo 3, Yecla • Map B4 • 968 79 11 15*

7 **Bodegas Salvador Poveda**
Pick up some of the famous Fondillón wine. *Ctra Monóvar Salinas, Km 3.2, Monóvar • Map D5 • 966 96 01 80*

8 **Bodegas Heretat de Cesilia**
Pay a visit to enjoy the fine wines and views of the vineyards. *Paraje Alcaydías 4, Novelda • Map D5 • 965 60 37 63*

9 **Cooperativa Virgen Pobre de Xaló**
Try the Mistela de Moscatel. *Crta Xaló (Jalón-Alcalalí), Xaló • Map G3 • 966 48 00 34*

10 **Bodegas 1890**
One of Spain's oldest wine producers. *Ctra de Murcia s/n, Jumilla • Map A4 • 968 75 81 00*

For more information on bodegas *visit www.winesfromspain.com*

Left **Aquopolis, Torrevieja** Right **Terra Mítica**

TOP 10 Family Attractions

Cuevas de Canalobre

1 Terra Mítica

The biggest, most exciting theme park on the Costa Blanca, Terra Mítica has everything from thrilling rollercoasters to huge waterslides. Each section is dedicated to one of the great Mediterranean civilizations, including the Romans, Greeks, Egyptians and Iberians. *Ctra Benidorm-Finestrat, Partida del Moralet s/n • Map F4 • 902 02 02 20 • Open summer: 10am–midnight daily; winter: 10am–8pm Sat, Sun. Closed Nov–mid-Mar • www.terramiticapark.com • Adm charge*

2 Cuevas de Canalobre

One of the biggest attractions on the Costa Blanca, this vast cavern, theatrically lit, gets its name from an amazing limestone outcrop in the form of a candelabra. *Xixona (Jijona) • Map E4 • 965 69 92 50 • Open Easter week and 1 Jul–15 Sep: 10:30am–7:30pm daily; 16 Sep–30 Jun: 10:30am–4:50pm Mon–Fri, 10:30am–5:50pm Sat, Sun • Adm charge*

3 Aquopolis, Torrevieja

This big, fun water-park has everything to keep the kids happy, from waterslides of all heights and shapes to wave pools and assorted swimming pools. There are special areas for toddlers, and plenty of snack bars and ice-cream shops. *Avda Delfina Viudes 99 • Map Q3 • 965 71 58 90 • Open mid-Jun–Aug: 11am–7pm daily; first two weeks Sep: 11am–6pm daily • www.aquopolis.es • Adm charge*

4 Mundomar, Benidorm

At this huge marine park, you can admire the flamingoes, penguins and turtles, or enter a spooky bat cave. Dolphins, sea lions and parrots perform spectacular shows. Other attractions include racoons and prairie dogs, and there's a special section for very young kids. *Sierra Helada s/n, Rincón de Loix, Benidorm • Map G4 • 965 86 91 01 • Open 10am–8:30pm daily • www.mundomar.es • Adm charge*

Dolphins at Mundomar, Benidorm

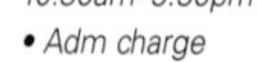

5 Safari Aitana, Penáguila

Tucked away in the Aitana Mountains, this safari park has lions, tigers, giraffes, elephants and more. There is a special section for smaller children, a restaurant, and a picnic area. *Ctra Alcoi Villa Joyosa Km 20, nr Penáguila • Map F3 • 965 52 92 73 • Open 11am–6:30pm daily • www.safariaitana.com • Adm charge*

6 Safari Park Vergel, Vergel (Verger)

Lions, tigers, wolves and leopards roam freely at this safari park. There are shows with parrots and sea lions, and a petting area with goats, pigs and ponies. *Ctra CV-700 Vergel–Pego • Map G2 • 966 43 98 08 • Open summer: 10am–7pm daily; winter: 10am–5pm daily • Adm charge*

7 Mundo Marino

One of the best ways to admire the stunning coastline is to take a ride in a glass-bottomed boat. This service offers full-day trips (including barbecues on board) from Denia (Dénia), Xàbia (Jávea), Calp (Calpe) and Altea. *Various departure points • Map H2, H3, G3, G4 • 966 42 30 66 • Times vary • www.mundo marino.es • Adm charge*

8 Pola Park, Santa Pola

This fun-park on the edge of Santa Pola has more than 20 attractions, including a roller coaster, pirate boats and other rides. *Avda Zaragoza s/n • Map E6, Q1 • 965 41 70 60 • Open mid-Mar–mid-Jun: 5–11pm Sat, 5–10:30pm Sun; mid-Jun–mid-Sep: 7:30pm–2am daily; mid-Sep–mid-Oct: 5:30pm–12:30am Sat, 5:30–11pm Sun (closed mid-Oct–mid-Mar) • www.polapark.com • Adm charge*

Mundo Marino boat trip

9 Terra Natura, Benidorm

Described as a "new-generation" wildlife park, Terra Natura has been designed to allow visitors to come into contact with the animals as if there were no barriers between them. The park is divided into four areas: Pangea, Asia, America and Europe. *Foia del Verdader 1 • Map G4 • 902 52 23 33 • Call ahead for opening hours • www.terranatura.com • Adm charge*

10 Karting La Cala

Kids (aged seven and over) will get a real kick out of this racetrack, one of the best karting circuits in Europe. The eight-minute slots are designed to test skill, speed and endurance. *Ctra Alicante-Valencia Km 116, nr Benidorm • Map F4 • 965 89 46 76 • Open summer: 10am–9pm daily; winter: 10am–5:30pm daily • Adm charge*

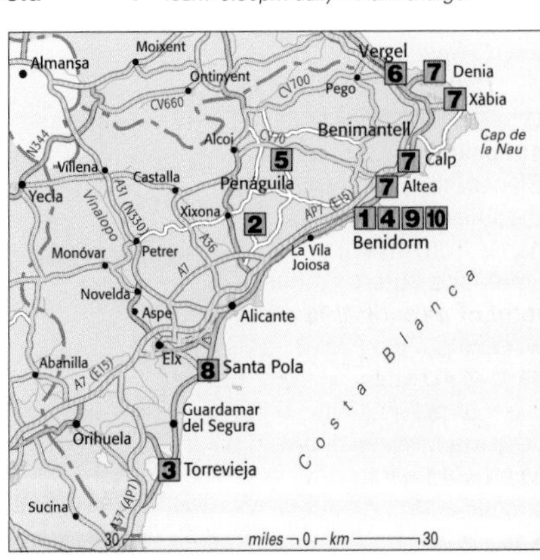

Left **La Puerta Falsa, Murcia** Right **Café del Puerto, Alicante**

Top 10 Nightspots

1 Old Town (El Barrio), Alicante (Alacant)

Every street in Alicante's atmospheric old quarter is packed solid with bars and nightclubs which start late and don't stop until dawn. There's a good mix of styles and places to go, with something to suit most tastes and age groups. *Map U2*

2 Café del Puerto, Alicante

Find a seat on the lovely open-air terrace overlooking the marina, and enjoy the view of Alicante's seafront. This is a great place to have a coffee or a gin and tonic before heading out for the evening. *Muelle de Levante s/n • Map V3 • Open from 3pm daily*

3 Tablao Zambra, El Campello

For a taste of Andalucía, make a date at the Tablao Zambra in El Campello, just up the coast from Alicante. The show is geared toward tourists, but the dancers and musicians are all incredibly talented. *C/San Pedro 61, El Campello • Map E5 • 965 63 23 10 • Open weekends (daily in summer) • www.tablaoflamencozambra.com*

4 C/Mallorca, C/Ibiza and C/Palma, Benidorm

Benidorm's nightlife is divided by nationality: these streets are the heart of the English section, and they are lined with British bars. Most offer karaoke, theme nights and other forms of entertainment. *Map G4*

Penélope Beach Club, Benidorm

5 Penélope Beach Club, Benidorm

One of the coolest clubs in Benidorm, with a perfect beachfront location, this is a great place to start the night. Top DJs, go-go dancers and a slick, well-dressed crowd. *Avda de Alcoi 10 • Map G4 • 965 86 33 60 • www.penelopebeach.com*

6 KM Disco, Benidorm

Featuring some of Spain's top DJs spinning everything from Spanish pop to the latest dance tracks, this is one of Benidorm's best-known mega-clubs. Also on this strip are Penélope, Pachá, and Manssion. *Ctra Alicante-Valencia Km 122 • Map G4 • 965 86 35 23 • www.kmdisco.com*

7 Pachá, Torrevieja

Music is provided by an excellent line-up of Spanish and European DJs at this outpost of the celebrated, international club, Pacha. A young crowd keeps the place buzzing until very late. *Avda Delfina Viudes • Map Q3 • 965 70 48 78 • www.pachatorrevieja.com*

For more nightspots **See pp76, 78, 90 & 108**

8 Zona de Las Tascas, Murcia

Murcia has a vibrant social scene centred around its university and party animals will be spoiled for choice in the Zona de Las Tascas area of the city. People of all ages gather around the streets near the Campus de la Merced to enjoy a drink and a bite to eat in the many bars and restaurants. Calle Enrique Villar and Calle San Ignacio de Loyola are right in the thick of the action. *Map U5*

9 La Puerta Falsa, Murcia

La Puerta Falsa is a classic on the Murcian music scene, a relaxed, bohemian spot which features live acts from Tuesday to Satuday nights. The music on offer spans everything from jazz, soul and blues to hip-hop and tango. There are also poetry readings and *tertulias* (discussion groups). *C/San Martín de Porres 5 • Map U4 • 968 24 86 51 • www.lapuertafalsa.com*

10 Revival, Alicante

Revival is one of the most popular discos on the "techno route" on the outskirts of Alicante, but be warned, it's for committed dance fans only; it keeps going non-stop from Saturday night right through until Monday morning. *Los Montesinos • Map E5 • 966 72 16 41 • www.discorevival.com*

Pachá, Torrevieja

Top 10 Tips for Clubbers

1 Don't Arrive Too Early
Be prepared for a late night; clubs in Spain rarely get going before 1am.

2 Dress to Impress
Take some trouble over your appearance; local clubbers make a big effort. Note that many clubs don't allow trainers (sports shoes).

3 Trensnochador
A special train service between Alicante and El Campello runs all through the night from Thursday to Saturday in July and August.

4 Free Drinks
Club admission prices usually include one drink, so make sure that you hang on to your ticket.

5 Flyers
You can get flyers on special one-off musical events from local music shops.

6 Terrazas
Many of the clubs on the Costa Blanca have outdoor terraces, which offer welcome respite from the rigours of the dance floor.

7 Proceed with Caution
Boys beware: Spanish women are usually surrounded by protective boyfriends or brothers.

8 Drugs
Drugs may well be offered to you, but they are illegal in Spain, and the penalties for possession are tough.

9 Special Events
You can get information about special events at www.clubbingspain.com (Spanish only).

10 Beach Parties
Beach parties are common, free and entirely spontaneous.

Left **Eating paella** Middle **The author enjoying a delicious orxata** Right **Oranges**

TOP 10 Culinary Highlights: Alicante

1 Paella

A genuine *paella* is made with round *bomba* rice (to soak up the stock), and delicately flavoured with garlic and saffron. Just before completion, the heat is turned up to create a light crust (*soccarat*). Everyone has their own recipe, which can include seafood, meat, vegetables or a mixture of all three.

2 Rice Dishes

Alicante is famous for the breathtaking variety of its rice dishes, ranging from the pungent *arroz negro*, cooked in squid ink, to *arroz a banda*, similar to *paella* and made with many different kinds of fish. (Dársena serves almost 200 types – *see p66*.)

3 Caldero

This rich stew, usually made with broth, rice and seafood, exists in many regional variations. One of the best known is the *caldero tabarquino*, a speciality of the Isla Tabarca *(see p24)*. Inland variations will often incorporate locally raised meat and game or flavoured sausage, and they are then called *gazpachos*.

4 Ollas

These traditional stews, named after the earthenware pot in which they are cooked, are common in the mountainous inland regions, particularly around Alcoi (Alcoy). Most *ollas* are made with whatever is available, but they usually contain dried beans, chickpeas (garbanzos) and root vegetables, and are flavoured with cured sausage.

5 Seafood

The abundance and variety of seafood on the Costa Blanca is astonishing. Fish is often simply grilled or fried, or used in the many rice dishes. *Dorada a la sal* (sea bream baked in rock salt) is common and delicious. Try Dénia's famous and very tasty prawns.

Arroz negro

6 Orxata (Horchata)

Orxata is a sweet, creamy drink made from ground tiger-nuts (*chufas*) – tastier and more refreshing than it might sound. Alicante produces a regional variation made with almonds. In summer, it's particularly delicious served with crushed ice *(orxata granizada)*. Look out for the sign *"artesanal"* – the home-made varieties are infinitely better than the bottled kind.

A selection of shellfish

7 Fruit and Vegetables

The Costa Blanca has long been known as the "orchard of Spain"; it produces vast quantities of fruit and vegetables, including oranges and lemons, the deliciously tart *nísperos*, almonds, olives and grapes. Head for any local market for a taste of the incredible variety on offer.

8 Alicantino Wine

Alicante's main wine-producing regions are around Monóvar and El Pinós *(see pp56–7)*, which make robust reds and a famous sweet dessert wine called El Fondillón. Teulada also produces good sweet dessert wines called *mistelas*.

Market stall, Elx (Elche)

9 Turrón

Anyone with a sweet tooth will be in heaven in the Costa Blanca, which is famous for *turrón*, the delicious local nougat made with honey and nuts. There are two kinds: a soft version called "Xixona" (Jijona), after the biggest producer of *turrón*, and a crunchier kind named "Alicante".

10 Chocolate

Chocoholics should head to the seaside town of La Vila Joiosa (Villajoyosa), which has been making chocolate for almost 300 years. A museum devoted to the subject is run by Valor (www.valor.es), one of the biggest chocolate-makers in Spain. Best of all, it offers tastings.

Top 10 Markets

1 Alicante (Alacant)

Alicante's Modernista-style market has all kinds of delicious fresh produce, and pretty flower stalls.

2 Santa Pola

Santa Pola holds a huge outdoor market on Saturdays, with everything from local produce to clothes and shoes.

3 El Campello

El Campello's fast and furious fish auction is held from 5pm Monday to Friday, and is open to the public.

4 Xaló (Jalón)

A market with interesting bric-a-brac is held every Saturday morning under the trees next to the river.

5 Xàtiva (Játiva)

A delightful, sprawling street market, with everything from curtains to socks, takes place in the old town on Tuesdays and Fridays.

6 Altea

An art market is held every evening during summer in the Plaza Iglesia at the top of the old village.

7 Benidorm

A big market is held every Wednesday in Benidorm, with lots of fresh food, as well as clothes and souvenirs.

8 Elx (Elche)

Famous for its palm grove *(see pp22–3)*, Elx holds its market on Mondays and Saturdays.

9 Gata de Gorgos

This market features local crafts (particularly wicker furniture – *see p74*), as well as food stalls.

10 La Nucía

This pretty village hosts a massive bric-a-brac market on Sunday mornings.

Left **Embutidos** Right **Orange tree in fruit**

TOP 10 Culinary Highlights: Murcia

1 Embutidos

Inland Murcia is celebrated for its cured pork sausages *(embutidos)*, including a dark blood sausage known as *morcilla*, as well as countless other types of varying spiciness and flavour. They are easily found in butchers' shops and markets, and regularly feature on the menu at tapas bars.

2 Empanadas

Empanadas, deliciously light pastry parcels stuffed with all kinds of fillings from tuna to ham, are common throughout Spain, but the best are made in Murcia. The perfect picnic dish, they are available in almost every bakery.

Empanadas

3 Seafood

Like so much of the Mediterranean coast, Murcia's fishing villages provide a wealth of wonderful fresh seafood. The famously sweet prawns from the Mar Menor, sea bream cooked in rock salt *(dorada a la sal)*, and a highly spiced version of the *caldero* *(see p62)* are all typical of the region.

Dorada a la sal

4 Moorish Sweets

The Arabic influence in Spain is all-pervasive – it's strongly felt even in Murcia's sweets and pastries. Try the caramelized almonds, the fresh *yemas* (made with egg yolks and lemon) – these are especially good around Caravaca de la Cruz – and *paparajotes*, exquisitely light lemon or orange pastries delicately flavoured with cinnamon. Irresistible!

5 Rice

Rice has been grown in the Calasparra region for more than a thousand years, and it now enjoys its own D.O. *(denominación de origen)*, which guarantees the quality. Most of the rice produced here is of the small, plump, *bomba* variety, which is often used in the traditional fisherman's stew *caldero. Bomba* rice is ideal, as it soaks up the fish broth to perfection.

6 Fruit and vegetables

The ghostly outlines of enormous greenhouses can be seen throughout much of the province. The main crops are tomatoes and capers (of which Murcia is the world's largest producer), but the fertile lands of the Segura and Ricote valleys produce a dazzling array of fresh fruit and vegetables, which always feature prominently in local dishes.

Every village will have its own local speciality – particularly the village bakeries.

7 Fritás de Moratalla

These are a delicious local variation of the popular Spanish *churros* (fried dough strips) – here they are sweetened with honey. You'll find them at stalls during all the local festivals, as well as in the cafés and cake shops around the sleepy hill village of Moratalla.

Ordering Fritás de Moratalla

8 Murcian Wine

Jumilla, Yecla and Bullas *(see p56)* have all been granted their own D.O., and produce a range of whites, reds and rosés. The powerful red wines, usually drunk young, are the best known outside of Spain, but Bullas is also notable for its refreshing rosés – perfect summer drinking.

9 Stews

Murcia has lots of wonderful traditional stews, including the *olla gitana*, a hearty chickpea and vegetable stew from the fertile Segura valley, and the *zarangollo murciano*, a tasty mixture of pumpkin, onion and tomato.

10 Meat and Game

Murcia's lush interior produces excellent local meat and game, and many dishes feature rabbit, hare, venison, partridge and quail. The most famous dish is *chuletas de cordero al ajo cabañil* – lamb chops served with a piquant dressing of garlic, vinegar and bay leaf.

Top 10 Murcian Meat Dishes

1 Pastel de Cierva
A traditional meat pie of veal, *chorizo*, egg, brains and minced meat, wrapped in pastry and baked in the oven.

2 Migas con Tropezones
Breadcrumbs fried with small pieces of pork – or with cured sausage.

3 Tartera Caravaqueña de Cordero
This lamb pie is a typical dish from Caravaca de la Cruz.

4 Pastel de Carne
A favourite from Murcia, this oven-baked pie is made with minced meat, tomato sauce and boiled egg. It is usually sold in bakeries.

5 Cordero Asado a la Murciana
A rustic dish of roast lamb with potatoes, parsley, garlic and pine nuts.

6 Gazpacho Jumillano
Murcian *gazpachos* are thick stews, unlike the popular chilled Andalucian soup of the same name. This one is made with rabbit and vegetables, and is served hot.

7 Cabrito en Salsa
Kid cooked with a piquant, garlicky sauce – popular in the northern sierras of Murcia.

8 Cordero en Pepitoria
Lamb's foot braised in a wine and herb sauce, delicately flavoured with saffron, bay leaves and parsley.

9 Empanada de Liebre, Arroz y Conejo
A hearty meat pasty made with chunks of hare and rabbit mixed with rice.

10 Perdiz con Judías
This local pheasant dish is cooked with beans, bay leaves and garlic.

Left **La Finca** Right **Palacete Rural La Seda**

Top 10 Restaurants

1 La Finca, Elx (Elche)

This beautiful restaurant surrounded by lush gardens offers traditional Mediterranean recipes with an innovative touch; the *menú degustación* will allow you to try a range of chef Susy Díaz's most popular creations. La Finca also boasts a fantastic wine cellar. *Partida Perleta 1–7 • Map D6 • 965 45 60 07 • Closed Sun D, Mon, last two weeks Jan, Easter • www.lafinca.es • €€€€*

2 El Poblet, Denia (Dénia)

Dynamic young chef Enrique Dacosta gives traditional rice dishes a highly creative twist at this excellent restaurant with a wonderful, breezy terrace. This is the very best place to try Denia's famous prawns, cooked to perfection. *Ctra Las Marinas Km 2.5 • Map H2 • 965 78 41 79 • Closed Sun D, Mon (except Aug), 3 weeks Feb–Mar • www.elpoblet.com • €€€€€*

3 Casa Pepa, Ondara

Set in a 140-year-old building surrounded by vegetable gardens, orange trees and olive groves, this restaurant is justifiably proud of its Michelin star. Booking ahead is essential. *Partida Pamís 7–30 • Map G2 • 965 76 66 06 • Closed Sun D, Mon • www.casapepa.es • €€€€*

Dársena

El Poblet

4 Hostería de Mont Sant, Xàtiva (Játiva)

Set in a charming small hotel in jasmine-scented gardens above the historic town of Xàtiva *(see p124)*, the restaurant specializes in traditional regional dishes, but the highlight is the romantic garden setting. *Subida al Castillo s/n • Map E1 • 962 27 50 81 • www.mont-sant.com • €€€*

5 Dársena, Alicante (Alacant)

With a perfect location on the port, Dársena resembles a great white ship, right down to its round windows and gleaming brass lamps. The speciality is rice; the menu offers almost 200 different rice dishes. The *arroz a banda* is particularly good. *Muelle de Levante 6 • Map E5 • 965 20 73 99 • www.darsena.com • €€€*

For a guide to restaurant price ranges **See p77**

6 Piripi, Alicante

Smart and stylish, Piripi serves some of the finest traditional rice dishes in the whole city. Try their delectable *arroz con sepionet y alcachofas* cooked with baby squid and artichokes, but be sure to save room for the delicious home-made desserts. The tapas bar is a local institution. *C/Oscar Esplá 30 • Map S3 • 965 22 79 40 • €€–€€€*

7 Casa Joaquín, Santa Pola

Not far from the port, this relaxed and informal little restaurant is wholeheartedly dedicated to seafood, and serves up whatever is freshest that day. You are in luck if the traditional fishermen's stew *caldero* is on the menu – the restaurant is said to make one of the tastiest versions around. *Plaza Félix de Rodríguez de la Fuente 9 • Map E6, Q1 • 965 41 12 82 • Open daily • €€€*

8 Rincón de Pepe, Murcia

The plushest restaurant in Murcia City, Rincón de Pepe serves exquisitely prepared fresh seafood from the Mar Menor (including cod in *pil-pil* sauce), as well as locally reared meats which are grilled to perfection. Old-fashioned in the best sense of the word, it offers impeccable service and a splendid, rather formal setting. *C/Apóstoles 34 • Map U6 • 968 21 22 39 • Closed Sun, Mon D • €€€€€*

9 Hostería Palacete Rural La Seda, nr Murcia

A beautiful 17th-century silk factory has been handsomely converted to house this elegant restaurant in a rural setting on the outskirts of Murcia City. The Palacete Rural La Seda uses the freshest local produce, including fruit and vegetables grown in its own orchard, as well as freshly caught seafood from the Mar Menor. *Vereda del Catalán s/n, Santa Cruz (8km from Murcia City) • Map N2 • 968 87 08 48 • Closed Sun & public hols • www.palacetelaseda.com • €€€€€*

Piripi

10 Porto Novo, Cartagena

This elegant restaurant overlooking Cartagena's marina is devoted to serving the freshest fish and seafood. It is also well known for the delicious rice dishes served at lunchtime and the evening *raciones* (large tapas) menu. *Paseo Alfonso XII • Map P5 • 968 52 87 93 • Closed Mon • €€€€*

For more places to eat See pp77, 79, 80, 91, 99, 107 & 109

AROUND COSTA BLANCA

Left **Xàbia (Jávea) town centre** Right **Denia (Dénia)**

Northern Costa Blanca

THE WINDSWEPT CAPES AND ENTICING COVES *of the northern Costa Blanca have attracted settlers for thousands of years, but the trickle became a deluge during the 1960s. It's easy to see the allure of the magnificent coastline, with its jagged cliffs and secret coves of turquoise water, but the coastal strip is only half the story. Just a few miles inland, remote sierras and lush valleys survive untouched, with whitewashed villages dreaming on hilltops, waterfalls plunging into natural pools, and ruined castles and ancient towns recalling an illustrious past.*

Penyal d'Ifac (Peñón de Ifach)

Top 10 Sights

1. **Gandia (Gandía)**
2. **Xàtiva (Játiva)**
3. **Vall de Gallinera**
4. **Denia (Dénia)**
5. **Xàbia (Jávea)**
6. **Penyal d'Ifac (Peñón de Ifach)**
7. **Guadalest**
8. **Parc de l'Aigüera, Benidorm**
9. **Callosa d'en Sarrià and Fonts d'Algar**
10. **Villena**

1 Gandia (Gandía)

Gandia's history is inextricably bound up with the Borjas; the opulent Gothic palace which was their family home has been impeccably restored *(see pp26–7)*. The only other reminder of the town's historic importance is the serene Gothic church of Santa María. A resort town, Gandía-Playa, has grown up around the port, with famously well-manicured beaches *(see p40)* and a buzzing nightlife scene in summer. ® *Map F2*

Xàtiva Castle

2 Xàtiva (Játiva)

This ancient mountain town is known as the "City of Two Popes" – Alexander VI and Calixto III (both Borjas) were born here. Piled steeply on a hillside, the narrow streets and arcaded squares are still scattered with handsome churches and escutcheoned mansions, which attest to its medieval importance. It's topped with a fine castle offering incredible views *(see also pp53, 55, 63)*. ® *Map E1*

3 Vall de Gallinera

The lush Gallinera Valley has been cultivated since Arabic times, and the hillsides are still lined with tidy stone terraces full of dusky olive groves and fruit orchards. The valley is scattered with tiny, ancient villages, their Arabic origins echoed in their names – Benialí, Benitaia, Benissivà – and reflected in the maze of crooked streets at their heart *(see also p42)*. ® *Map F2*

Orange groves outside Denia

4 Denia (Dénia)

Now a popular family resort, Denia was once a substantial Roman settlement. There's a lofty castle, and a charming old quarter huddled around the port, but Denia's most popular attractions are still its lengthy beaches: the long, family-friendly sands to the north, and a pretty, cove-pocked stretch called Les Rotes to the south *(see p40)*. The strange, bald peak of Montgó looms above the town, perfect for hiking and picnicking *(see pp36, 42)*. ® *Map H2*

5 Xàbia (Jávea)

Xàbia's bay is perfectly caught between two dramatic capes: the Cap de Sant Antoni and the Cap de la Nau *(see pp36, 75)*. The old village of Xàbia, a whitewashed huddle of impossibly narrow streets around a fortified medieval church *(see p53)*, is set back from the lively modern resort which has grown up around the bay. ® *Map H3*

Guadalest

6 Penyal d'Ifac (Peñón de Ifach)

This huge, jagged rock emerges dramatically from the sea and dominates the entire bay at Calp (Calpe). A protected Natural Park, it is home to over 300 species of flora. Connected to the mainland by a narrow isthmus, and impossibly sheer, for centuries it was the perfect hideout for pirates. Now it provides the perfect challenge for rock-climbers and, thanks to a tunnel bored through the rock early in the last century, there's also a less arduous (though still demanding) hiking route to the top *(see pp16–17)*. ✆ *Map G4*

7 Guadalest

Perched high on a crag in a sea of mountain peaks, the little whitewashed village of Guadalest is huddled under the ruins of an ancient castle. Once it was a strategic military outpost, but it lost its importance after earthquakes devastated the region and irreparably damaged the castle. Thanks to its stunning location and the picturesque charm of its old-fashioned lanes and squares, Guadalest is now the most visited village in Spain. Quirky museums, cafés and souvenir shops have sprung up, but although tour buses disgorge an endless stream of visitors in summer, Guadalest has hung onto its medieval tranquility and charm. ✆ *Map F3*

The Lovelorn Giant

There's a curious notch "missing" from the spiky mountains behind Benidorm. According to legend, it was torn out and tossed into the bay by a despairing giant who had been told that his beloved would die by the time the sun set. In so doing he gave her a few moments more of life; the rock became the Isla de Benidorm *(see p36)*.

8 Parc de l'Aigüera, Benidorm

In a town best known until now for cheap sun, sea and sand *(see p38)*, the Parc de l'Aigüera is a landmark new development. Designed by prestigious Catalan architect Ricardo Bofill, this vast, urban park spreads north of the old village of Benidorm. It draws on Classical influences, with an elegant avenue bordered by a stepped terrace decorated with vast urns. This culminates in a circular outdoor amphitheatre, surrounded, Roman-style, with stepped seating. Concerts take place here during the summer months, but it's always a quiet place for a stroll, a world away from the bedlam on the beach-front. ✆ *Map G4*

9 Callosa d'en Sarrià and Fonts d'Algar

The most interesting thing about the modest little village of Callosa d'en Sarrià is actually just outside of it. In a pretty, orchard-filled valley (from Callosa take the road to Tárberna and follow the signs) are the Fonts d'Algar, a lovely cascade of waterfalls and natural swimming pools set among shady forest *(see pp36, 42)*. Several excellent walking trails lead from here to the Sierra de Bernia *(see p43)*. *Map G3*

10 Villena

The large, prosperous town of Villena is crowned by a storybook castle, complete with hefty, crenellated walls and watchtowers. At its feet lies a chaotic sprawl of tile-roofed houses, the heart of the medieval village. The central Plaza de Santiago is surrounded by handsome 16th-century palaces and the graceful Renaissance church of Santa María, which bears a flamboyant Baroque façade. The finest palace on this square is now the town hall, home to an archaeology museum which contains the sumptuous Tesoro de Villena, a spectacular hoard of Bronze Age gold discovered by chance in the 1960s *(see p54)*. *Map C4*

Tesoro de Villena (Villena Treasure)

A Morning in Xàtiva

This walk is best done on a Tuesday or Friday, when the market is held. A **castle** has sat on the lofty promontory above the town of Xàtiva since Iberian times. Start your morning – before the sun gets too hot – with the stiff climb up to the castle (sign-posted "castell"), or take the easy option of the little tourist train which runs from outside the tourist office. From the castle ramparts, the lovely old city unfolds at your feet, surrounded by endless sierras. One of the finest and most complete castles in the region, this is a sublime setting for a music festival held every summer.

On the way down, you can stop for refreshment in the gardens of the charming **Hostería de Mont Sant** *(see p124)*. When you reach the main town, continue down Calle las Santas and turn right onto Calle Roca for the **Museo de l'Almudí** *(see p55)*, with an excellent collection of archaeological finds and paintings (including some by Xàtiva-born artist José de Ribera). If you are here on market day, head down to the nearby **Plaza del Mercado,** where stalls selling everything from clothes to pots and pans are set out under ancient arcades. Walk up to the Calle Corretgeria and visit the huge **Colegiata de Santa María** *(see p53)*, still unfinished after more than 400 years. Opposite the basilica is the beautiful **Hospital Real** (now local administration offices), with a dazzling, exquisitely sculpted Gothic façade. For lunch, try the traditional **Casa La Abuela** (C/Reina 17; 962 28 10 85).

Left **Ceramics in Altea** Right **Wickerwork in Gata de Gorgos**

Top 10 Shopping Towns

1 Altea
The pretty village of Altea *(see pp38, 63)* was "discovered" by artists during the 1960s and '70s, and is filled with galleries and craft shops selling everything from watercolours to pottery and hand-made jewellery. *Map G4*

2 Xixona (Jijona)
Xixona *(see p48)* is the biggest producer of the delicious Spanish nougat *(turrón)*, which is traditionally eaten at Christmas but is available all year round at countless local shops. *Map E4*

3 Ibi
Ibi's long toy-making tradition is sadly now being supplanted by cheap plastics, but you can still pick up pretty replicas of old-fashioned tin toys at the delightful Museu Valencià del Joguet *(see p55)*. *Map E4*

4 Gata de Gorgos
The little inland village of Gata de Gorgos is crammed with shops devoted to traditional wicker and straw crafts, from garden furniture to straw baskets and wonderful floppy hats. *Map G3*

5 Ontinyent
The delightful mountain town of Ontinyent has been producing textiles since Arabic times, and its high-quality wool blankets are exported all around the world. There are numerous factory outlets offering excellent bargains. *Map E2*

6 Alicante (Alacant)
In this medium-sized town *(see pp10–13 and 83)* shoppers can find anything from clothes and souvenirs, to typical Spanish foodstuffs and well-made leather goods. *Map E5*

7 La Vila Joiosa (Villajoyosa)
La Vila Joiosa *(see pp38, 63)* has been making chocolate since the 17th century. You can buy the perfect souvenir at the famous Valor chocolate factory on the outskirts of town. *Map F4*

8 Alcoi (Alcoy)
Alcoi *(see pp48, 50)* is famous in the region for traditional sweets first introduced by the Arabs. Most cake shops sell sugared almonds and the tasty sugar-coated pine nuts called *peladillas*. *Map E3*

9 Benidorm
Brash, brazen Benidorm *(see pp38, 40)* is the place to go if you're looking for kitsch souvenirs. It's also a great place to find cheap t-shirts and a huge variety of beachwear to suit all tastes and budgets. *Map G4*

10 Guadalest
Guadalest *(see pp14–15)* is packed with souvenir shops, offering delicate, handmade lace tablecloths, woollen blankets, slippers and traditional capes. You'll also find a good range of local produce, from liqueurs to honey. *Map F3*

Left **Picnic area, Banyeres de Mariola** Right **Cap de la Nau**

TOP 10 Views and Picnic Spots

1 Barranc de la Encantà
The track for the Barranc de la Encantà is signposted just before Planes. It twists crazily down to the "Enchanted Ravine", a perfect picnic spot, where a waterfall tumbles into a natural swimming pool. *Map F3*

2 Adzubieta
The romantic dry-stone ruins of this ancient Arabic village close to Alcalà de la Jovada in the Vall de Gallinera are great for picnics. A stiff path leads to the rocky peak of La Foradada for fantastic views. *Map F3*

3 Peak of Montgó
If you take the long but not too arduous trail through Montgó Natural Park *(see p36)* to the top of the mountain, you will be rewarded with gorgeous views over the scrubland and rugged cliff. *Map H2*

4 Cap de Sant Antoni
The lighthouse at the tip of the windy Cape of Sant Antoni affords gorgeous views over wave-battered cliffs and the pretty resort of Xàbia (Jávea) curled around the bay. *Map H2*

5 Cap de la Nau (Cabo de la Nao)
Rounding off the southern end of the bay at Xàbia, the Cap de la Nau *(see p36)* is dotted with well-marked *miradors* (viewing points). The Portitxol *mirador* is especially lovely. *Map H3*

6 Embalse de Guadalest
This huge, deep blue reservoir at the foot of the valley overlooked by the picturesque village of Guadalest is a wonderful place to stop for a picnic after a hard morning's sightseeing. *Map F3*

7 Banyeres de Mariola
There is a lovely picnic and camping area on the outskirts of Banyeres, on the road to Biar. From there you can enjoy great views over the village and its Arab castle *(see p47)*, or take a stroll along the river. *Map D3*

8 Jardín de Santos, Penáguila
These immaculate 19th-century gardens in pine woods on the edge of the dreamy mountain village of Penáguila are the idyllic setting for a popular barbecue area with picnic tables. *Map F3*

9 Xàtiva (Játiva) Castle
Xàtiva's lofty castle offers beautiful views over the tranquil mountain town, with its tiled rooftops and slender spires, and out across endless mountains fading into the distance. *Map E1*

10 Penyal d'Ifac (Peñón de Ifach) summit mirador
The *mirador* at the summit of the Penyal d'Ifac *(see pp16–17)* is the ultimate viewing point – but you'll have to work to get there, as it's a stiff and slippery 45-minute climb from the base. *Map G4*

KM Disco

TOP 10 Benidorm Nightlife

1 Lennon's
Lennon's is a big favourite with the under-25s, and the dance floor (playing high-energy dance music) is always heaving at weekends. *C/Mallorca • Map G4*

2 Churchill's
A favourite with the Brits, this brash, raucous pub hosts legendary karaoke nights which pack in the punters, plus theme nights and lots of competitions. Tacky but fun, in true Benidorm style. *C/Lepanto 14 • Map G4*

3 Penélope Beach Club
The beachfront outpost of the mega-club Penélope, this is an elegant bar-cum-club, where you can sip a cocktail and watch the crowds flow along the seafront. The action starts late, when the music hots up and the go-gos get going *(see p60)*.

4 KM Disco
KM is one of several mega-clubs on the Carretera Alicante-Valencia (others include Pachá, Manssion and Penélope). It has room for 5,000 people and boasts spectacular laser shows. The wristband issued to you on entry gives you free access to all other mega-clubs *(see p60)*.

5 Daytona
This motorcycle bar is right on Levante Beach and serves up American cuisine as well as live rock music from afternoons until late. *Av Alcoi s/n • Map G4*

6 Benidorm Palace
Come here for the biggest, flashiest and most extravagant shows in town, with acrobats, cabaret singers and show girls. *Avda Severo Ochoa 13 • Map G4 • 965 85 16 60 • www.benidorm-palace.com*

7 KU Playa
A classic in Benidorm, KU Playa is definitely one of the top places to see and to be seen. *Avda Alcoi 6 • Map G4 • 965 85 29 27*

8 Sinatra's
This celebrated cocktail bar features regular cabaret acts and other live performances (usually in winter), and attracts a more mature clientele. *C/Mallorca • Map G4 • 966 80 73 80*

9 Hotel Babylon
Benidorm has a buzzing gay scene, and there are many places to choose from. The bar at this basic hotel located in the heart of the Gay Village is a good venue for meals throughout the day, but especially suited for a pre-clubbing drink in the evening. *C/Alicante 28 • Map G6 • 966 88 95 60 • www.babylonbenidorm.com*

10 Fratelli Fashion Bar
The name of this club couldn't be more appropriate. The chic, modern interior attracts a very fashionable crowd, who cruise in to drink and pose. *C/ Doctor Orts Llorca, Edificio Principado Arena • Map H6 • 965 85 39 79 • www.fratellibar.com*

Three lively streets – C/Mallorca, C/Ibiza and C/Palma – form the hub of Benidorm's hectic nightlife.

La Rana

Price Categories

For a three course meal for one with half a bottle of wine (or equivalent meal), taxes and extra charges.

€	under €20
€€	€20–€30
€€€	€30–€40
€€€€	€40–€50
€€€€€	over €50

TOP 10 Benidorm Cafés and Restaurants

1 Art a la Cucina

One of the smartest places to dine in Benidorm, this restaurant, which opened in 2005, offers traditional recipes with a contemporary twist. It also has an excellent *bodega* and a *menú del día* at lunchtime. *Avda Marina Baixa, Local 5 • Map F6 • 965 86 63 16 • www.artalacucina.com • €€€€*

2 Sorrento Trattoria

Classic Italian cuisine is on the menu at this popular restaurant. Their wide-ranging selection of pizzas is a firm favourite with the locals. *Avda Estocolmo 22 • 965 85 94 13 • €€€*

3 Say Yes

If you are looking for light refreshments, then the teas and salads in this welcoming lounge café might be right up your street. *Avda Severo Ochoa s/n • Map G4 • 965 85 32 82 • €*

4 Easo Berri

All kinds of delicacies from the Basque lands are on offer at this upmarket tapas bar, including excellent shellfish, best washed down with a typically crisp Basque white wine. *C/Santo Domingo • Map G4 • 965 86 43 50 • €€*

5 Casa Toni

This smart restaurant serves impeccable local rice and seafood dishes, but it's the tapas bar which really pulls in the crowds. *Avda Cuenca, Edificio Gemelo 4 • Map G4 • 966 80 12 32 • Closed Sun D, Mon • €€€*

6 La Cava Aragonesa

There are dozens of tapas bars along the Calle Santo Domingo. This one serves a huge range and is incredibly popular as a result, so expect to find standing room only. *C/Santo Domingo • Map G4 • 966 80 12 06 • €€*

7 L'Albufera

L'Albufera covers all bases with lots of tapas plus an array of excellent local rice dishes. It offers a good value fixed-price menu at lunchtimes, and, unusually, in the evenings too. *C/Girona 3 • Map G4 • €€*

8 Aitona

One of the best places to try an authentic *paella*, this brightly lit eaterie is a favourite with locals and tourists alike. It also serves tasty, simply grilled local meat. *C/Ruzafa 2 • Map G4 • 965 85 30 10 • €€*

9 La Rana

A popular tapas bar in the old quarter, with a wide variety of delicious tapas to sample. Wash down with a robust local wine. *Costera del Barco 6 • Map G4 • 965 86 81 20 • Closed Sun • €€*

10 Ulía

Always busy thanks to its perfect seafront location, Ulía serves up simply prepared fresh fish and authentic local rice dishes like *arroz a banda* on its breezy terrace. *Avda Vicente Llorca Alos 12 • Map G4 • 965 85 68 28 • €€€*

"Tapas Alley" runs from Plaza de la Constitucíon and along Santo Domingo.

La Plaza

Top 10 Nightlife

1 La Plaza, Altea
Live jazz, blues and soul are sometimes on the programme at this mellow cocktail bar on the prettiest square in the village. *Plaza de la Iglesia 12 • Map G4 • 965 84 26 30*

2 Blues, Denia (Dénia)
Located near Las Rotas beach, opposite the wharf, Blues offers live music and a welcoming atmosphere. The bar is popular with locals and tourists alike. *Ctra Denia-Xàbia 3 • Map H2 • 965 78 46 16*

3 Café del Sol, Denia
Relax and enjoy a drink at this lovely pub facing Denia's pretty harbour. *Explanada Cervantes s/n • Map H2*

4 Bacarrá, Gandia (Gandía)
Bacarrá's "disco-garden" is the place to be during the hot summer months. There are all kinds of events, from DJs to live gigs, go-go dancers and special one-off theme parties. *C/Legazpi 7 • Map F2 • 962 84 02 58 • www.discotecabacarra.com*

5 La Hacienda, Xàbia (Jávea)
This club is always packed on summer weekends. As well as offering house, soul and funk music, La Hacienda is the perfect place to watch the sunrise after a hard night's clubbing. *Ctra Cabo de San Antonio • Map H3 • www.discotecahacienda.com*

6 Cocoon, Altea
Situated in the Old Town of Altea, with magnificent views over the sea, Cocoon offers a pleasant mix of chill-out and dance music. *Plaza de la Iglesia • Map G4 • 966 88 16 56 • www.cocoonlounge.com*

7 Albades, Alcoi (Alcoy)
This huge club has three spaces: "Auditorio Underground" for the latest dance music; "Vanguard Music" for techno and house; and "Exitos" for pop. *Ctra Nacional 340 s/n • Map E3 • 966 51 64 02 • www.albades.com*

8 Olé, Xàbia
This taverna is more than a tapas bar. Housed in a handsome 19th-century mansion, there are always temporary art exhibitions, and live music (usually jazz or blues) throughout the summer months. *C/San Buenaventura 9 • Map H3 • 966 46 23 76 • www.bar-ole-javea.com*

9 La Llum, Xàbia
House and techno keep the party going until dawn at La Llum, another of Xàbia's popular discos. *Carrer de Gual 1 • Map H3*

10 Palau Altea, Altea
Altea's main cultural centre features regular performances of opera, *zarzuela* (typical Spanish operetta), theatre dance and classical music, as well as jazz, flamenco and pop concerts. *C/Alcoi 18 • Map G4 • 966 88 19 24 • www.palaualtea.com*

La Capella

Price Categories

For a three course meal for one with half a bottle of wine (or equivalent meal), taxes and extra charges.

€	under €20
€€	€20–€30
€€€	€30–€40
€€€€	€40–€50
€€€€€	over €50

Top 10 Places to Eat

1 Casa Pepa, Ondara
The dining rooms of this Michelin-starred restaurant are stylishly decorated, and the gardens are spectacular *(see p66)*.

2 El Poblet, Denia (Dénia)
Try fresh seafood (including Denia's famous prawns) and local rice dishes, imaginatively prepared at this excellent restaurant *(see p66)*.

3 L'Escaleta, Cocentaina
This elegant chalet at the foot of the mountains serves elaborate regional cuisine – succulent lamb, exquisitely fresh fish, heavenly desserts. There are beautiful mountain views from the terrace. *Subida Estación Norte 205 • Map E3 • 965 59 21 00 • Closed Sun D, Mon, 2nd two weeks Jan • €€€*

4 Restaurante Mistral, Oliva
This charming traditional restaurant, with beautiful views of the surrounding orange groves, serves cod and duck dishes but specializes in *paellas* and other rice dishes. *Partida Elca s/n • Map G2 • 962 85 53 49 • Closed D, Mon (Sep–Jun), L (Jul, Aug) • €€*

5 La Bohême, Xàbia (Jávea)
The selection of fresh tapas is the speciality at this popular seaside spot; there's also a range of fresh seafood and simple meat dishes to choose from. *Paseo Amanecer • Map H3 • 965 79 16 00 • €€*

6 La Capella, Altea
Dine under vine-draped arches on the terrace of this charming restaurant. There are good traditional dishes, as well as a selection of tapas at the popular bar. *C/San Pablo 1 • Map G4 • 966 88 04 84 • Closed Wed • €€€*

7 Warynessy, Villena
Sleepy Villena is an unlikely setting for this sleek restaurant and bar, which serves modern versions of traditional Alicantino recipes, and wonderful desserts. *C/Isabel la Católica 13 • Map C4 • 965 80 10 47 • Closed Mon • €€€*

8 Hostería de Mont Sant, Xàtiva (Játiva)
This excellent restaurant serves traditional regional dishes on a pretty garden terrace *(see p66)*.

9 El Viscayo, Castalla
This friendly country eatery makes its own *embutidos* *(see p64)*, and is famous for its delectable *gazpachos*, a shepherd's dish made with meat and game, and served with flatbread. *Camino la Bola s/n • Map D4 • 965 56 01 96 • Closed D • €€*

10 Ca L'Ángeles, Polop
This welcoming restaurant set in an old house in the pretty village of Polop serves fresh fish and authentic local dishes like kid with roasted garlic. *C/Gabriel Miró 12 • Map G4 • 965 87 02 26 • Closed mid-Jun–mid-Jul; also D except Fri, Sat (Sep–mid-Jun), Tue (mid-Jul–Aug) • €*

Left **Isla Tabarca** Right **Dunas de Guardamar**

Southern Costa Blanca

ALICANTE (ALACANT), CAPITAL OF THE COSTA BLANCA, *boasts an enticing old quarter piled chaotically around the lower slopes of a vast cliff, where a magnificent fortress has stood guard for 1,000 years. Modern avenues are packed with fantastic shopping, and the* tapeo *(a bar crawl between tapas bars) is an institution. Inland, parched plains give way to mountains riddled with caves and scattered with medieval villages and ancient castles, which recall the region's position on the front line between the Arabic and Christian worlds during the Middle Ages. The modest town of Novelda is the unexpected setting for an architectural gem from the more recent past. Along the coastline, long, sandy beaches make up for the lack of dramatic scenery, and you can escape the crowds on the lovely island of Tabarca. Heading south, the elegant town of Elx (Elche) is surrounded by ancient palm groves first established by the Phoenicans, and Orihuela's affluent and aristocratic history is recalled by a beautiful ensemble of Gothic churches and Renaissance palaces.*

The beach at Santa Pola

Top 10 Sights

1. Alicante (Alacant)
2. Santa Pola
3. Isla Tabarca
4. Elx (Elche)
5. Orihuela
6. Dunas de Guardamar
7. Torrevieja
8. Petrer (Petrel)
9. Cuevas de Canalobre
10. Novelda

Preceding pages **The Vall de Guadalest**

1 Alicante (Alacant)

The main gateway to the Costa Blanca, this bustling city is often overlooked in the charge to the beaches and resorts, yet this is one of Spain's most engaging cities, with a picturesque old quarter, beautiful churches and fascinating museums, and a lively port with plenty of bars and restaurants. The city is dominated by the splendid Castillo de Santa Bárbara, high on a cliff above the sea *(see pp10–13)*. *Map E5*

2 Santa Pola

Santa Pola is a cheerful family resort set around a pretty port. At the heart of the village is a sturdy castle built in the 16th century as a defence against pirates. The lighthouse at the tip of the Cape of Santa Pola offers fine views of the coastline and out to the small island of Tabarca, a short ferry-ride away. The salt lakes on the fringes of the village are now a Natural Park attracting flamingoes and other aquatic birds. *Map E6, Q1*

3 Isla Tabarca

The island of Tabarca *(see pp24–5)*, 2 km (1 mile) long and 450 metres (492 yards) wide, sits just off the coast of Santa Pola. Wild, pebbly coves and delightful little bays pucker its shoreline, and the clear waters have been designated a marine reserve. All year round, regular ferries make the short journey from Santa Pola. Ferries also run from Alicante, Benidorm and Guardamar (ask at local tourist offices for timetables). Many tourists simply make for the seafood restaurants around the port, leaving the little town to more intrepid explorers. *Map E6*

Alicante's *Ayuntamiento* (town hall)

4 Elx (Elche)

The immaculate town of Elx is best known for its celebrated palm groves, introduced by the Phoenicians more than two millennia ago, and in particular for the "Priest's Garden" *(see p22–3)*, a luxuriant botanical garden filled with palms and tropical flowers. Most of the town's historic sights are clustered around the Basílica de Santa María, the setting for the Misteri d'Elx *(see pp50, 52)*. Both the Misteri d'Elx and the palm grove have been declared UNESCO World Heritage sites. An Iberian settlement, Illici, is being excavated on the outskirts of Elx; it is here that the famous Dama de Elx, the most accomplished Iberian sculpture in Spain, was found. The MAHE Museum *(see p54)* is another interesting option. *Map D6, Q1*

Cactus Garden, Hort del Cura, Elx

Torrevieja's promenade

5 Orihuela

Magnificent churches, monasteries and palaces attest to Orihuela's distinguished history. Set back from the coast in a fertile valley and surrounded by rolling sierras, this ancient capital of an Arabic *taifa* became an important centre of learning after the Reconquest *(see p34)*, and the Catholic monarchs held court here before making the final push on the last Arabic kingdom of Granada. The narrow streets are lined with faded palaces and countless fine churches, including the graceful cathedral, the Colegio de Santo Domingo *(see p52)* and the utterly charming Iglesia de Santas Justa y Rufina. *Map P2*

6 Dunas de Guardamar

This wild and lovely stretch of windswept dunes on the outskirts of the low-key tourist enclave of Guardamar is a protected area, which has blocked the intrusion of the kind of high-rise developments that have blighted other parts of the coast. The dunes undulate along endless beaches of fine pale sand, backed by shady pine glades with walking paths, cycling routes, archaeological remains and picnic areas. Although the beaches are very popular in summer, they remain relatively uncrowded. Nonetheless, the best time to visit is off-season, when you can go for long, bracing beach walks without a soul in sight. *Map Q2*

Empress Sisi

The Imperial Palm in Elx's Hort del Cura is named in honour of the Empress Sisi of Austria (1837–98). She was the Princess Diana of her time, a beautiful and tortured figure who escaped the stifling responsibilities of court life by sailing around the Mediterranean, and indulging in bizarre beauty treatments, which included bathing in cow's milk.

7 Torrevieja

This substantial resort town packed with villas and second homes has a lively seafront promenade and unusual rock pools in place of a beach. There's also a huge modern marina offering plentiful facilities for sailing and other watersports. There are ranks of bars and restaurants to choose from. On the fringes of the town sit two vast salt lakes, with gleaming pyramids of freshly formed salt – a designated nature reserve that attracts several species of birds, both migratory and resident. *Map Q3*

8 Petrer (Petrel)

Medieval Petrer is dominated by its impressive castle *(see p47)*. The old town has almost been swallowed by the adjacent (and unlovely) industrial city of Elda, which is squeezed right up to its borders. Both towns share a long shoe-making tradition, and Petrer's narrow streets are still home to traditional cobblers. There's a pretty Neo-Classical church and a pair of charming hermitages. *Map D4*

9 Cuevas de Canalobre

This vast cavern, which soars up for almost 140 m (460 ft), is the largest and most impressive of a network of caves which riddle the Cabecó d'Or mountain near Busot. It was probably first discovered by the Arabs, and has been put to all kinds of strange uses, including housing a factory for aeroplane engines during the Spanish Civil War *(see p58)*.

Cuevas de Canalobre

10 Novelda

Sleepy Novelda rarely makes it onto tourist itineraries, but it should. This charming if rather dilapidated little country town boasts a cluster of fine Modernista mansions, of which the most impressive is the Casa-Museo Modernista *(see pp18–19)*. On the edge of town, the castle of La Mola squats next to the Gaudí-inspired sanctuary of Saint Mary Magdalene. *Map D5*

A Day in Two Cities

Morning

Allow a full day (Tue to Sat) for this tour of two elegant but very different cities. Begin in **Orihuela**, at the **tourist office**, housed in a splendid Baroque palace on Calle Francisco Die. Peek into the Gothic **church of Santiago** before doubling back to the delightful **church of Santas Justa y Rufina**, with its unmistakable bell tower. The Calle Santa Justa leads into the Calle Ramón y Cajal, lined with terrace cafés and shops, where the graceful **Catedral de San Salvador** overlooks a pretty square. Continue west to the vast **Colegio de Santo Domingo**, topped with a pastel tower seemingly made of icing sugar. Head back into the historic centre for lunch at **Casablanca** (C/Meca 1; 965 30 10 29), which serves delicious, hearty traditional stews.

Afternoon

Take the short drive along the A7 motorway to **Elx**, set in famous palm groves. Explore the **Hort del Cura** *(see pp22–3)*, then stroll back to the historic heart of the town and the vast blue-domed **Basílica de Santa María**. Next to the basilica is a 13th-century watchtower, the **Torre de la Calaforra**. You can learn more about the famous Misteri d'Elx, the last surviving medieval mystery play in Europe, at the nearby **Museo de la Festa** on Carrer Major de la Vila. Finish up with a well-earned drink on the terrace of the **Café Paris** (Plaza del Congreso Eucarístico) overlooking the basílica.

Left **Dates on market stall in Elx (Elche)** Right **Monóvar**

Top 10 Shopping Towns

1 Agost

Agost's long ceramic-making tradition dates back for centuries, and dozens of shops sell the earthenware water jars *(botijos)* typical of the region, along with a range of ceramic items from pots to platters. *Map D5*

2 Alicante (Alacant)

The ultimate one-stop shopping destination, Alicante has the biggest department stores, plus plenty of large high-street chain shops, all lined up along the Avenida Maisonnave. *Map E5*

3 Elda

Elda is a big, industrial city, and one of the largest shoe-making centres in Spain. Numerous factory outlets on the outskirts of the town offer excellent shoe bargains. *Map D4*

4 El Pinós (Pinoso)

El Pinós is one of the best-known wine towns in the Alicante region *(see p57)*, but it's also justly famous for its *embutidos* – cured hams and sausages made with locally reared livestock and prepared to traditional recipes. *Map C5*

5 Crevillent

Crevillent has dozens of workshops and factories offering the luxurious and colourful rugs and carpets for which it is renowned throughout Spain. Other local crafts include glass-ware and wickerwork. *Map D6*

6 Elx (Elche)

Come around Easter to see Elx's famous and elaborate palm crosses being made for the Palm Sunday parades *(see pp22–23)*. At any time of year, dozens of shops sell fresh dates and delicious date sweets and cakes. *Map D6, Q1*

7 Santa Pola

Santa Pola's traditional souvenirs are objects made from seashells – a fashion which you may have thought died out in the 1970s. These run the gamut from the kitsch to the surprisingly pretty. *Map E6, Q1*

8 Torrevieja

Torrevieja is edged with two enormous salt lakes, and its pale pyramids of gleaming salt make a curious sight. In town, souvenir shops sell unusual carved boats made entirely from salt. *Map Q3*

9 Novelda

Novelda *(see pp18–19, 85)* is most famous for its marble, but if that proves difficult to pack, you could pick up some locally grown golden saffron to flavour your own *paellas (see p62)* instead. *Map D5*

10 Monóvar

The cheerful wine town of Monóvar *(see p56)* produces an excellent, robust red wine, as well as rosés, but it is best known for the wonderful dessert wine El Fondillón. *Map D5*

Left **Picnic, Castillo de Santa Bárbara, Alicante** Right **View from the Tryp Gran Sol, Alicante**

TOP 10 Views and Picnic Spots

1 Petrer (Petrel) Castle
The most impressive of a line of castles which cuts through the middle of the Alicante region, the sturdy fortifications of Petrer Castle make for a perfect picnic – and, indeed, picture – spot with endless views. *Map D4*

2 Tibi Reservoir
This remote reservoir near the village of Tibi is formed by the oldest working dam in Europe, built at the end of the 16th century, and perfectly slotted into a narrow gorge. *Map E4*

3 Castillo de Santa Bárbara, Alicante (Alacant)
Alicante's spectacular hilltop castle *(see pp10–11)* dominates the whole city, and its ramparts and terraces offer endless views over the deep blue Mediterranean. *Map V2*

4 Dunas de Guardamar
The protected expanse of undulating dunes *(see p41)* backed by a gnarled pine forest on the edge of Guardamar del Segura makes a delightful place for a picnic. *Map Q2*

5 Isla Tabarca
The secluded coves at the western end of this pretty island *(see pp24–5)* are perfect for picnics. If you need to work up an appetite, you can always go swimming or snorkelling first. *Map E6, R1*

6 Parque Municipal, Elx (Elche)
This delightful palm-shaded park with ceramic-tiled benches is right in the heart of town. The children's play areas make it perfect for family picnics. *Map D6, Q1*

7 Castillo de la Mola, Novelda
This lofty castle, squeezed up against an extraordinary Modernista sanctuary *(see p47)*, offers far-reaching views across endless plains and a strange lunar landscape of abruptly jutting peaks. *Map D5*

8 Faro de Santa Pola
Santa Pola's lighthouse, right out at the tip of the cape, is a wonderful place to come at dusk, with views out across the cliffs to the diminutive island of Tabarca. *Map E6, Q1*

9 Tryp Gran Sol, Alicante
The panoramic restaurant on the 26th floor of the Tryp Gran Sol Hotel in Alicante serves good regional dishes against the fabulous backdrop of the yacht-filled port and the sea. *Rambla de Méndez Núñez 3 • Map U3*

10 El Palmeral, Orihuela
After a busy morning's sightseeing around the historic city of Orihuela *(see p84)*, the delightful and extensive palm grove on the edge of town makes a refreshing change and is perfect for picnics. *Map P2*

Left **Turrones Teclo** Right **Mango**

TOP 10 Alicante Shops

1 El Corte Inglés
Alicante has two branches of El Corte Inglés, Spain's biggest department store. The groceries are excellent, if expensive. *Avda Maisonnave 53 • Map T3 • 965 92 50 01*

2 Zara
Zara, one of the best-known Spanish chains, offers catwalk fashions at affordable prices. Men, children and babies are also catered for, and there's a new line of stylish things for the home. *Avda Maisonnave 42–44 • Map T3 • 965 92 37 41*

3 Mango
This well-known Spanish chain has stylish clothes, shoes and accessories for women, with everything from fashionable suits for the office to jeans and funky clubwear. *Avda Maisonnave 33–39 • Map S3 • 965 12 54 87*

4 FNAC
At this popular book, music and electronic gadget superstore, you can sit in a quiet corner and read one of the latest bestsellers, or listen to one of the many CDs they have on offer. *Avda Estación 5–7 • Map S3 • 966 01 01 00*

5 Turrones Teclo
This delightful, old-fashioned shop on the main street of the old quarter sells different varieties of the delicious local nougat, *turrón*, which makes a great gift for the sweet-toothed. *C/Mayor 23 • Map U2 • 965 20 11 15*

6 Turrones Espí
Espí, one of the best *turrón* producers from Xixona, has a small, exclusive shop in Alicante where you can buy their products. *C/Tomás López Torregrosa 17 • Map U2 • 965 21 44 41*

7 Enoteca Bernardino
Choose from over 2,500 wines, including an excellent regional Spanish selection, as well as imported wines from France, Chile and Argentina. *C/Alberola 38 • Map E5 • 965 28 08 73*

8 Explanada Street Market
Canopied white stalls line Alicante's famous promenade, selling jewellery, ceramics, beachwear and more besides. Many open during the day, but the market is liveliest on summer evenings. *Map U3*

9 Mercado Central
This delightful Modernista market is surrounded by colourful stalls selling fresh flowers. Inside, you'll find fabulous heaps of fruit, vegetables, fish and meat. It's a great place for picnic supplies. *Avda Alfonso X el Sabio • Map T2*

10 Flors i Fulles
This charming flower shop creates beautiful bouquets, but it also sells attractive gifts for the home and garden – vases, glassware, plant pots and other ceramics. *C/Bailén 21 • Map U3 • 965 21 26 22*

Restaurante Ibéricos

Price Categories

For a three course meal for one with half a bottle of wine (or equivalent meal), taxes and extra charges.

€	under €20
€€	€20–€30
€€€	€30–€40
€€€€	€40–€50
€€€€€	over €50

TOP 10 Alicante Tapas Bars

1 Nou Manolín

Upstairs is one of the best restaurants in Alicante *(see p91)*. Downstairs, the exceptional range and quality of the tapas means it's usually standing room only at the bar. *C/Villegas 3 • Map U2 • 965 20 03 68 • Restaurant: €€€€; tapas bar: €€*

2 La Taberna del Gourmet

This atmospheric tapas bar on a lively street is permanently packed. It serves a great array of fresh tapas, accompanied by an excellent wine list featuring lots of good local wines. *C/San Fernando 10 • Map T3 • 965 20 42 33 • €€€*

3 Restaurante Ibéricos

The dangling hams signal this restaurant's speciality. A whole section of the menu is dedicated to ham, but there are plenty of other dishes to choose from. *C/Gerona 5 • Map U3 • 965 21 30 08 • Closed Sun • €€€*

4 Guillermo

This sweet little tapas bar is a neighbourhood favourite, serving tasty, traditional tapas and a refreshingly crisp local white wine. *C/Pintor Velázquez 21 • Map T2 • 965 20 01 84 • Closed Sun • €*

5 O'Pote Gallego

Seafood is the speciality here, cooked to traditional Galician recipes. It's a cosy spot, with a permanent knot of locals at the bar. *Plaza Santa Faz 6 • Map U2 • 965 20 80 84 • Closed Mon • €€*

6 Govana

Join the locals at this busy place for great fish and meat dishes, or try their excellent selection of rice dishes. *Plaza Dr Gómez Ulla 4 • Map S3 • 965 21 82 50 • Closed D • €€€*

7 Mesón Labradores

Complete with colourfully tiled walls and a stack of wine barrels, this classic tapas bar in the heart of the old quarter serves an extensive menu of traditional tapas. *C/Labradores 19 • Map U2 • 965 20 48 46 • Closed Mon (except eve of bank hols) • €€*

8 Buen Comer

This long-established café-bar in the old quarter serves good tapas and *raciones* downstairs; upstairs, there's a fancier restaurant, with delicious seafood and rice dishes. *C/Mayor 8 • Map U2 • 965 21 31 03 • €–€€*

9 Mesón Rias Baixas

This family-run restaurant and bar is always packed to the rafters. The tapas are some of the best in town. Try the melt-in-the-mouth octopus cooked Galician-style. *C/Pablo Iglesias 15 • Map T2 • 965 20 37 69 • Closed Sun D, Tue • €€*

10 Taverna Ibérica

Tucked away in a quiet street in the Old Town, this great restaurant serves a range of typical regional dishes and delicious tapas. *C/Toledo 18 • Map U2 • 965 21 62 58 • Closed Sun D, Mon • €€*

Many restaurants also have tapas bars – for example, Piripi (see p67).

Left **Pachà discoteca** Middle **Celestial Copas** Right **Casino de Torrevieja**

TOP 10 Nightlife

1 Clan Cabaret, Alicante (Alacant)

An Alicante classic, with live performances, poetry readings, *tertulias* (discussion groups) and temporary art exhibitions, Clan Cabaret is a great place to relax in the evenings. *C/Capitán Segarra 16 • Map T2 • 965 21 00 03 • www.clancabaret.com*

2 Celestial Copas, Alicante

Possibly the most eccentric bar in Alicante, Celestial Copas has a wacky, enjoyably kitsch decor. Flamenco, rumba and *sevillanas* for an older crowd. *C/San Pascual 1 • Map U2*

3 Nic, Alicante

Located in a pedestrianized street in the city centre, this elegant cocktail bar is the perfect place to start the evening. *C/Castaños 22 • Map U2 • 965 21 63 20 • www.nicalicante.com*

4 Z Klub, Alicante

This big, slick disco just off the lively Calle San Fernando is currently one of the most fashionable in Alicante (as the admission price of €10 reflects). An enthusiastic crowd dances to the latest house and techno tunes. *C/Coloma 3 • Map U3*

5 Tablao Zambra, El Campello

A genuine corner of Andalucía on the Costa Blanca, the Tablao Zambra in El Campello (a few miles up the coast from Alicante) features flamenco music and dance by gifted Andalucian performers *(see p60)*.

6 Pachá, Torrevieja

There's an outpost of Pachá in almost every party town on the Med; this one attracts Spanish and international DJs, who keep the lively young crowd dancing until dawn *(see p60)*.

7 Mr Frog Bowling, Elx (Elche)

For a family night out, try this big bowling alley, which has a café and an amusement arcade with slot machines. *C/Murcia 1 • Map D6, Q1 • 966 61 14 75*

8 Casino de Torrevieja

Torrevieja's splendid Modernista casino *(see p48)* is open for members only, but anybody can visit the cafeteria for a drink.

9 Camelot, Santa Pola

This beachside club with an outdoor dance area is a classic on the summer nightclub scene. Spanish pop is interspersed with house and techno. *Gran Playa • Map E6, Q1 • www.clubcamelot.com*

10 Sperantto, Alicante

Thanks to its splendid location facing El Postiguet beach, this bar is busy at any time of the day or night. Simple lunch and dinner menus are also available. *Playa Postiguet, Bajo Hotel Meliá • Map V3 • 965 21 74 88*

La Sirena

Price Categories

For a three course meal for one with half a bottle of wine (or equivalent meal), taxes and extra charges.

€	under €20
€€	€20–€30
€€€	€30–€40
€€€€	€40–€50
€€€€€	over €50

Top 10 Places to Eat

1 Piripi, Alicante (Alacant)
One of Alicante's finest restaurants, this is a great option if you want to try the local rice dishes. The tapas bar is one of the best in town *(see p67)*.

2 Nou Manolín, Alicante
Excellent rice dishes (including a spectacular *arroz a la banda*) are on offer at this welcoming restaurant, with an elegant whitewashed dining room upstairs and a fantastic tapas bar downstairs *(see p89)*.

3 La Sirena, Petrer (Petrel)
Its elegant decor and magnificent regional cuisine have made La Sirena one of the top restaurants in the Costa Blanca. There's an affordable lunchtime *menú del día*. *Avda de Madrid 14 • Map D4 • 965 37 17 18 • Closed Mon, Sun D, Easter wk, 3 wks Aug • €€€€€*

4 Los Barriles, Orihuela
This charming, rustically decorated tavern has been dishing up delicious seafood specialities for more than a century. *C/La Sal 1 • Map P2 • 966 74 23 65 • Closed Sun, Aug • €€*

5 Restaurante Parque Municipal, Elx (Elche)
This pretty, pavilion-style restaurant in the heart of Elx's palm grove serves traditional rice dishes and seafood. Try the *arroz con costra* – a meaty rice dish with baked eggs. *Parque Municipal, Paseo de l'Estació • Map D6 • 965 45 34 15 • €€*

6 Casa Paco, Guardamar del Segura
This relaxed, family restaurant with a huge terrace is a favourite with locals and tourists alike. *C/Mediterráneo 14 • Map Q2 • 966 72 55 56 • Closed Mon in winter • €€*

7 La Almadraba, Isla Tabarca
Traditional restaurant with a pretty terrace overlooking the port. The menu offers plenty of local dishes, including *caldero tabarquino* *(see p24)*. *C/Virgen del Carmen 29 • Map E6 • 965 97 05 87 • Closed D • €€*

8 Batiste, Santa Pola
This big, airy seafood restaurant sits right on the port, so you know the fish is fresh. All kinds of shellfish are on the menu, along with tasty rice specialities. *Avda Fernando Pérez Ojeda 6 • Map E6 • 965 41 14 85 • €€€*

9 Nou Cucuch, Novelda
This traditional restaurant and tapas bar is one of the best in town. *Pasaje Isidro Seller 8 • Map D5 • 965 60 15 00 • Closed Mon–Thu, Sun D • €€€*

10 Xiri, Monóvar
Set in a fragrant park, Xiri offers sophisticated Mediterranean cuisine with an Oriental twist (for example, langoustine salad with sesame dressing). Finish up with one of their spectacular desserts. *Parque Alameda s/n • Map D5 • 965 47 29 10 • Closed Sun D, Mon, 3 wks from mid-Jun • €€€*

Left **Islands of the Mar Menor** Right **Águilas**

Costa Cálida

THE SUN SHINES, ON AVERAGE, FOR 300 DAYS OF THE YEAR *on Murcia's "Warm Coast", which stretches from Europe's largest saltwater lagoon, the Mar Menor, down to the wild and rocky coastline around Águilas. If you're a watersports enthusiast, look no further than La Manga. But venture south and you'll find, among other delights, the Regional Park of Calblanque, one of the most beautiful stretches of coastline on the Mediterranean; the spectacular scenery of the Cabo Tiñoso; and Cartagena, the region's largest city, where Roman and Carthaginian ruins rub shoulders with Modernista mansions.*

Calblanque

TOP 10 Sights

1. **Mar Menor**
2. **Santiago de la Ribera**
3. **Cabo de Palos**
4. **La Manga del Mar Menor**
5. **Calblanque**
6. **Cartagena**
7. **Puerto de Mazarrón**
8. **Ciudad Encantada de Bolnuevo**
9. **Parque Natural de Calnegre y Cabo Cope**
10. **Águilas**

1 Mar Menor

The Mar Menor is the largest saltwater lagoon in Europe, with more than 70 km (43 miles) of coastline. Relatively shallow, with a maximum depth of 7 m (23 ft), it's always several degrees warmer than the nearby Mediterranean, and its high salt content makes it easier to float in. Rich in minerals, it has been reputed since Roman times to cure all kinds of ills. The sea is strewn with volcanic islands: Isla Barón is the largest, but pretty Isla Perdiguera is the focus of most boat trips – and a great place to try some freshly caught seafood. *Map P4*

2 Santiago de la Ribera

This plush, modern resort on the shores of the Mar Menor boasts an excellent marina and a long, palm-lined seafront promenade. Like so many resorts on the Mediterranean coast, this was once a humble fishing village, and a few colourful fishing boats are still drawn up on its sandy beaches. The tranquil waters of the Mar Menor are ideal for anyone learning to sail or windsurf, and there are excellent facilities for watersports. Ferries regularly sail for Isla Perdiguera. *Map P4*

3 Cabo de Palos

Inhabited since Roman times, Cabo de Palos sits right at the southernmost tip of the long spit separating the Mar Menor from the Mediterranean. An imposing lighthouse offers spectacular views of both seas and the rocky coastline. Despite the influx of tourism, the village has hung onto its long fishing tradition, and trawlers rub shoulders with yachts and gin palaces in the harbour. You'll find plenty of good seafood restaurants here, but the star attraction is the proximity of the wild and beautiful Regional Park of Calblanque *(see pp8–9)*. *Map Q5*

The port of Cabo de Palos

4 La Manga del Mar Menor

La Manga – "The Sleeve" – is the name given to the curious, long spit of land which divides the Mar Menor from the Mediterranean. The entire 21 km (13 miles) length is now densely packed with a virtually unbroken line of brash high-rise apartment buildings and hotels, a mini-Manhattan which is visible for miles around. Dedicated entirely to summer fun, the beaches are lined with bars, cafés and restaurants, and offer numerous opportunities for all kinds of watersports, including windsurfing, waterskiing, fishing and sailing. Regular ferries ply between La Manga and the islands of the Mar Menor. *Map Q4*

La Manga del Mar Menor

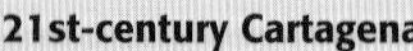

21st-century Cartagena

Until recently, Cartagena was a ghost town living on memories of its illustrious past. But a huge injection of cash has meant a spectacular flowering of glossy museums, glassy modern architecture, a spanking new marina, and a facelift for the once-neglected Roman ruins and florid Modernista buildings, like the opulent *Ayuntamiento* (city hall).

5 Calblanque

The Regional Park of Calblanque has one of the most beautiful stretches of coastline in the region, with crystal-clear waters perfect for snorkelling and diving. Behind the shore lie pine-clad mountains, with excellent walking and mountain-biking trails *(see pp8–9).*

6 Cartagena

Founded by the Carthaginians in the 3rd century BC, resettled by the Romans, and beloved by the Arabs, Cartagena has had a long, dramatic history. The old town is peppered with Roman ruins and overlooked by a hilltop castle, which offers panoramic views over the sprawling city and out to sea. The Calle Mayor is still lined with flamboyant Modernista mansions, the legacy of a 19th-century boom. The city's long naval history is recounted in the fascinating Museo Nacional de Arqueología Subacuática. *Map P5*

Roman ruins, Cartagena

7 Puerto de Mazarrón

The modest resort of Puerto de Mazarrón, one of the most southerly on the Costa Cálida, is popular with Murcian families. An attractive fishing port and marina sit side by side at the foot of a jutting cape; around it spread low-key developments and long beaches of dark sand interspersed with rocky coves. The resort is linked to the village of Mazarrón, with a smattering of historic monuments, including the Modernista town hall and the pretty 16th-century church of San Andrés. *Map M5*

8 Ciudad Encantada de Bolnuevo

The little fishing village and tourist resort of Bolnuevo boasts a fine, dark sandy beach and a series of beautiful coves to its south, reached by a winding road which hugs the cliff. These secret coves are well off the beaten track, and as a result they are popular with naturists. Behind the main beach is the Ciudad Encantada, an "enchanted city" of bizarre rock formations eroded by the wind and sea into extraordinary shapes. You can enter this strange, pale city and watch the rocks melt magically into faces, cathedrals or animals as you pass between them. *Map M5*

9 Parque Natural de Calnegre y Cabo Cope

As you progress to the southernmost tip of Murcia's Costa Cálida, the terrain becomes increasingly wild and rocky. This hauntingly lovely cape is now a protected Natural Park, and home to all kinds of birds and animals, including wild boar, sea turtles, cormorants and peregrine falcons. Footpaths are traced through the scrub, and you can climb up to the summit of the cape for stunning views of the sheer cliffs and the wheeling seabirds. In the lee of the cape is a dramatic stretch of rocky inlets and coves, perfect for a dip, overlooked by a 16th-century watchtower built to defend the coast from pirates. *Map L6*

Parque Natural de Calnegre y Cabo Cope

10 Águilas

Nudged up against the border with Andalucía, this quiet resort curls around a broad sandy bay, with spectacular rocky capes at either end and a scattering of volcanic islands rising abruptly from the sea. The delightful port sits at the foot of a steep cliff at the southern end of the bay; it's full of working fishing boats, which supply delicious fresh fish to the local restaurants. The Castle of San José, beautifully flood-lit at night, looms dramatically from the clifftop. In February, the town hosts one of the biggest carnivals in Spain. *Map L6*

A Drive on the Costa Cálida

Morning

Start the day with coffee at one of the beachfront bars on the promenade at **Águilas**, then head 3 km (2 miles) north out of the town, past the pretty harbour of Calabardina, to **Cabo Cope**. Climb the 16th-century watchtower, and splash about in the rock pools along the beach.

Return toward Águilas, but take the signposted turning for Garrobillo. The road twists along the mountainous fringes of the Natural Park, providing startling glimpses of the sea. It becomes even more dramatic once you reach Garrobillo, when the road narrows further and zigzags furiously toward Humbrías. When it joins the N332, turn left and stop for lunch at the fantastic roadside **Bar Surtidor** (Ctra Mazarrón-Águilas Km 15, just before the turning for Cañada de Gallego), a classic country café with a spectacular array of tapas.

Afternoon

Continue past vast tomato greenhouses toward Mazarrón. As you approach the town, follow signs for the Gredas de Bolnuevo. The little resort of **Bolnuevo** is strung out along a fine, sandy beach, where you can have your second swim of the day. Behind it is the extraordinary "Enchanted City". If you really want to escape the crowds, explore the quiet coves south of town.

For dinner, head to the port in **Mazarrón** for delicious seafood at **El Puerto** *(see p99)*.

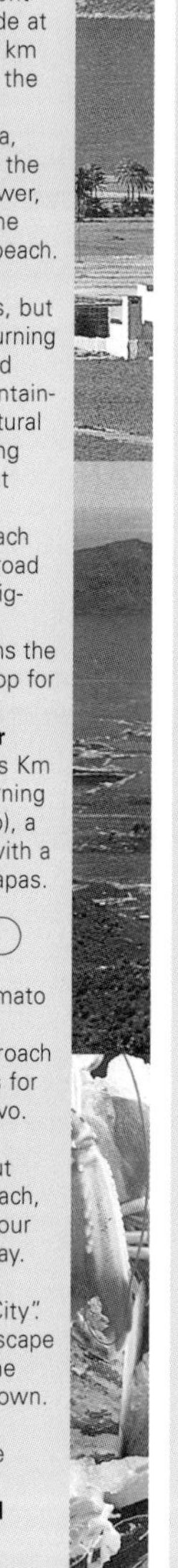

Left **Cabo de Palos** Right **Águilas**

Top 10 Lighthouses

1 La Manga
Almost at the tip of "the sleeve" (La Manga), this enormous lighthouse sits above the biggest marina on the Mar Menor, and looks out over the Mediterranean and a pair of miniature islands. *Map Q5*

2 Cabo de Palos
The view from the huge lighthouse overlooking the fishing village of Cabo de Palos is very different depending on which way you face: on one side, you'll see the Mediterranean crashing dramatically on the cliffs; on the other, the tranquil waters of the Mar Menor. *Map Q5*

3 Cartagena
One of the biggest ports in Spain, Cartagena is spread around a huge natural bay. Its sturdy red-brick lighthouse keeps watch over the endless flotillas of container ships. *Map P5*

4 Islas Hormigas
These tiny, rocky islets off Cabo de Palos are topped by another lighthouse – a beautiful sight at dusk. *Map Q5*

5 Punta Negra
Perched over a tiny bay with unusual dark sand, this lighthouse stands at the western end of the beautiful Regional Park of Calblanque *(see pp8–9)*. Walking trails splinter off in all directions, and there's a spectacular hike along the cliffs. *Map P5*

6 Islas de Escombreras
A few islets are strewn around the entrance to the enormous port at Cartagena; a lighthouse, visible from the cape below Escombreras, gives early warning to ships. *Map P5*

7 Cabo Tiñoso
A straggling dirt track leads to the lighthouse at the tip of this wild and beautiful headland, gazing out over crashing waves, long fingers of rock, and tiny, hidden bays. *Map N5*

8 Puerto de Mazarrón
The family resort of Puerto de Mazarrón is sprawled around a rugged, cove-studded cape. A dusty path wriggles to the top for beautiful sea views from the lighthouse. *Map M5*

9 Punta del Poniente
The coastline gets wilder as it heads down the Costa Cálida. The lighthouse at the tip of the Punta del Poniente (north of Águilas) keeps watch over sheer cliffs and scores of tiny islands. *Map L6*

10 Águilas
Águilas's lighthouse stands guard at the southern end of the bay, near the town's pretty fishing port. Painted in black and white stripes, it looks like something out of a storybook. To complete the picture, above it looms the dramatic castle. *Map L6*

Left **Windsurfing** Right **Fishing**

TOP 10 Sports Facilities

1 Diving

Most of the resorts on the Mar Menor, as well as the southern resorts of Puerto de Mazarrón and Águilas, have a number of companies offering diving courses, excursions and equipment hire. Tourist offices can provide lists.

2 Snorkelling

The endless coves of the coastline (Águilas alone boasts 35) are perfect for snorkelling, but the very best place to try it is the Regional Park of Calblanque, where the protected waters are clear and the bays are secluded.

3 Sailing

The Mar Menor is famous for its many marinas and excellent sailing facilities. The tranquil inland sea is ideal for beginners, and there is plenty to keep experienced sailors happy on the Mediterranean side of La Manga.

4 Windsurfing

Sailboards for windsurfing can be hired at almost every beach on the Mar Menor. Beginners will find the quiet inland sea a good place to learn; more advanced windsurfers can brave the Mediterranean.

5 Fishing

Fishing is very popular in Spain, but permits are usually required. Tourist information offices or local fishing tackle shops can provide information.

6 Golf

The famous La Manga Club *(see p44)* has three championship courses, open to all on payment of green fees. The nearby Las Lomas Village and Spa *(see p130)* also has a golf course.

7 Horse Riding

There are several stables around the Mar Menor, including a number in Los Belones offering treks around the Regional Park of Calblanque *(see pp8–9)*. Tourist offices will have the details.

8 Tennis

Many of the larger hotels around the Mar Menor boast tennis courts, and will usually let non-residents play for a fee. Most of the larger towns along the coast have municipal courts, which can be hired through the local tourist information office.

9 Hiking

The Natural Park of Calnegre and Cabo Cope has some good hiking, but the very best walking trails can be found in the Regional Park of Calblanque. A long-distance walking path, the GR92, runs the whole length of the Costa Cálida.

10 Bird-watching

The salt lakes in the Regional Park of Calblanque attract numerous birds, as do the protected salt flats around Lo Pagán, on the northern shores of the Mar Menor.

There are few surfing spots on the Costa Blanca, but experienced surfers should head for the Regional Park of Calblanque.

Left **Fuente de Cope** Right **Bolnuevo**

TOP 10 Beaches

1 Calblanque
The beaches of the Regional Park of Calblanque are the best in the whole of the Costa Cálida. Choose from sandy stretches, or discover your own private cove *(see pp8–9)*. *Map P5*

2 Calabardina
Tucked around a tiny bay with crystal-clear waters, pretty little Calabardina is a charming and barely developed resort, boasting several quiet beaches and rocky coves. *Map L6*

3 Fuente de Cope
Near the watchtower in the Natural Park of Calnegre y Cabo Cope *(see p95)*, this is a wonderfully unspoilt stretch of coastline, with rocky outcrops and pools sheltered by the impressive cape. *Map L6*

4 Bolnuevo
Bolnuevo's long, sandy beach is backed by surreal rock formations *(see p37)*, and has plenty of cafés and other facilities. To really get away from it all, head south down the coast, where there are dozens of secret coves. *Map M5*

5 Portús
Tucked in the lee of a rocky headland south of Cartagena, this narrow pebbly beach is well off the beaten track. There are little bays to be discovered, and it's an authorized nudist beach. *Map N5*

6 Punta Negra
Escape the crowds in this tiny cove near the ghostly former mining town of Portmán. The shingled beaches are dotted with upturned boats. Nearby, there's excellent walking in the Regional Park of Calblanque. *Map P5*

7 Playa Honda
One of the most popular beaches on the Mar Menor, the Playa Honda is a wonderful 7-km (4-mile) stretch of sand around Mar de Cristal, with every imaginable facility. *Map Q5*

8 Águilas
The elegant curve of Águilas's bay is broken by strangely shaped volcanic islands, perfect for snorkelling. Long, fine sands and plenty of amenities have made it extremely popular with families. *Map L6*

9 Santiago de la Ribera
The main beach of this upmarket resort is backed by a wooden, palm-shaded boardwalk and the long sandy expanse is lined with countless bars and cafés. It's particularly good for families. *Map P4*

10 Cala del Pino
On the Mar Menor side of La Manga, this popular beach with fine sand looks out over the islets dotting the inland sea. All kinds of facilities (including a marina) are close at hand. *Map Q4*

Restaurante La Tana

Price Categories

For a three course meal for one with half a bottle of wine (or equivalent meal), taxes and extra charges.

€	under €20
€€	€20–€30
€€€	€30–€40
€€€€	€40–€50
€€€€€	over €50

TOP 10 Places to Eat

1 Restaurante El Hijo del Rubio, Lo Pagán

This elegant restaurant serves up a fabulous selection of fresh seafood and fish, as well as good paella and *caldero (see p62).* *Explanada de la Feria s/n (inside El Club Náutico) • Map P4 • 968 18 18 07 • Closed Wed & Nov • €€€*

2 El Puerto, Puerto de Mazarrón

Right on the port, this popular local restaurant specializes in seafood. The *caldereta de langosta*, a delectable stew made with local prawns, is wonderful. *Plaza del Mar • Map M5 • 968 59 48 05 • Closed Mon in winter • €€*

3 La Meseguera de Los Porches, Puerto de Mazarrón

Sample mouthwatering paellas and other regional cuisine in this inviting restaurant. Excellent fresh fish. *Avenida Antoñita Moreno 56 • Map M5 • 968 59 41 54 • Closed Thu, winter • €€€*

4 El Faro, Águilas

Stylish, friendly and popular with a younger crowd, El Faro serves tasty local dishes at very reasonable prices. *C/José María Pereda s/n • Map L6 • 968 41 28 83 • Closed Tue & Wed D • €€*

5 Porto Novo, Cartagena

Devoted to fish and seafood dishes, this restaurant offers a great location and views over the marina *(see p67).*

6 La Tartana, Cartagena

This elegant restaurant serves a fantastic selection of the freshest fish and meat. The *menú del día* is a bargain. There's also a busy tapas bar. *Puerta de Murcia 14 • Map P5 • 968 50 00 11 • Closed Sun in summer • €€€*

7 Las Brisas, Águilas

Decked out like a ship, Las Brisas specializes in fish. It serves a good lunchtime *menú del día* – the only time you'll find their excellent *paella* on the menu. *Explanada del Puerto s/n • Map L6 • 968 41 00 27 • Closed Mon, Sun D • €€€*

8 Restaurante La Tana, Cabo de Palos

Good seafood and rice dishes are served at this popular restaurant. The house speciality is *arroz la Tana*, a succulent stew of squid and shrimp. *Paseo de la Barra 33 • Map Q5 • 968 56 30 03 • Closed Dec • €€*

9 El Mosqui, Cabo de Palos

Excellent *caldero (see p62)* and fabulously fresh *pescado frito* (fried fish platter) at this popular dining spot with a nautical feel. *Subida al Faro 50 • Map Q5 • 968 56 45 63 • Closed L & Thu in winter • €€*

10 La Casa del Reloj, San Pedro del Pinatar

This beautiful 19th-century mansion contains several elegant dining spaces set around a patio, and a piano bar. Particularly good rice dishes. *Las Plazas s/n • Map P3 • 968 18 24 06 • Closed Wed & Nov • €€€*

Left **Balneario de Archena** Right **Jumilla Castle**

Inland Murcia

MURCIA IS SPAIN AT ITS MOST AUTHENTIC AND UNSPOILT. *Enchanting villages spill down hillsides topped with ruined castles bequeathed by the soldier-knights who ruled here after the Reconquest; verdant fields and orchards recall the Arabs who first cultivated these lands. The Romans brought the vine, and wine is still produced in the charming wine towns of Jumilla, Bullas and Yecla – the perfect accompaniment to the robust mountain cuisine served in countless country restaurants. Wild sierras fan out to the furthest corners of the province; the loveliest of them all, the magnificent Regional Park of the Sierra de Espuña, is a stunning, forested mountain range, scattered with ancient snow wells, and home to a wonderful variety of animal and bird life. Murcia City bursts with extravagant Baroque churches and palaces, and its sumptuous cathedral* (see pp28–29)*, 400 years in the making, is one of the finest in Spain.*

Town Hall, Murcia City

TOP 10 Sights

1. Murcia City
2. Archena
3. Jumilla
4. Caravaca de la Cruz
5. Moratalla
6. Calasparra
7. Mula
8. Lorca
9. Aledo
10. Sierra de Espuña

Preceding pages **Typical Spanish fans on a flea market stall**

1 Murcia City

The welcoming capital city of Murcia Province is a delightful mix of the old and the new, with flamboyant Baroque churches, elegant modern shopping avenues, flower-filled public squares and gardens, and intriguing museums all clustered together in the old centre *(see p30)*. The magnificent Baroque Cathedral of Santa María *(see pp28–9)* is one of the loveliest in all Spain. The graceful squares are packed with excellent tapas bars and restaurants. *Map N3*

Jumilla

2 Archena

There is little to see in the sleepy market town of Archena besides the florid Baroque Church of San Juan Bautista and a few neglected aristocratic mansions, but its spa (Balneario de Archena) has been famous since Roman times. Prettily located in a cool palm grove on the banks of the River Segura, the spa has grown into a miniature village, complete with a delightful chapel and 19th-century casino. There are three hotels *(see p128)*, and a whole range of health and beauty treatments are on offer. *Map M2*

3 Jumilla

Jumilla, an unassuming country town piled chaotically on a hillside, is surrounded by endless vines *(see p56)*. The Romans first introduced wine to the area almost 2,000 years ago, and it has been produced here ever since. You can find out about its history in the local Museo del Vino, or take a tour of the *bodegas* for a taste of what's on offer. The old town has a pair of pretty churches and an unusual palaeochristian funerary monument, and is crowned by Jumilla's much-restored 15th-century castle, which offers panoramic views of the vine-covered plain and distant sierras. *Map A4*

4 Caravaca de la Cruz

The golden town of Caravaca de la Cruz is spectacularly set among the rugged sierras of northeastern Murcia. After the Reconquest, the town passed to the Knights Templar, who built the handsome castle, which still dominates the town. This contains Caravaca's greatest treasure, the Santuario de la Vera Cruz, which houses a relic of the True Cross, brought here, according to legend, by two angels in 1231. The miracle is commemorated annually on 3 May, when the relic is processed through the streets. A handsome ensemble of medieval and Renaissance mansions and churches are clustered in the old town. *Map K2*

Caravaca de la Cruz

La Virgen de la Esperanza

A shepherd discovered the "Virgin of Hope" in a cave near Calasparra, but the tiny statue miraculously grew too heavy to lift when the townspeople came to transfer it to a church. The sanctuary they built over the cave has been the focus of popular pilgrimages ever since, and the Virgin remains one of the most venerated in Spain.

5 Moratalla

Medieval Moratalla is a tawny huddle of stone houses steeply piled around a sturdy castle. A traditional mountain town with few monuments, Moratalla's greatest charms are the natural beauty of the surrounding sierras and its tranquil pace of life, which continues much as it has for centuries. The local cuisine is traditional, with hearty stews and plenty of grilled meat and game. The festivals, particularly Easter Week, are celebrated in old-fashioned style. On Maundy Thursday and Good Friday, the town resounds to the sound of almost a thousand drummers making their way through the centre of town. *Map K1*

Lorca

6 Calasparra

Calasparra overlooks a lush valley on the banks of the River Segura; settlers have been drawn to this area since neolithic times. During the Middle Ages, it was an important frontier settlement controlled by the Order of the Knights of Malta, who built its 13th-century castle. Now, it's a serene agricultural town surrounded by a sea of blossom in spring, and golden rice fields in the autumn. Rice dishes feature prominently on local menus *(see p64)*, along with pungent cured sausages and hams. *Map K1*

7 Mula

Mula is clamped to a steep hillside beneath the impressive ruins of a 16th-century castle. The intricate maze of winding streets and passages at the heart of the old quarter recalls the town's Arabic origins. Here you will find faded mansions and elaborate churches, many built under the auspices of the Marquises of Vélez during the 16th century, when Mula enjoyed its greatest period of prosperity. On the fringes of the town, the delightful spa at Baños de Mula has been famous since Roman times. *Map L2*

8 Lorca

Lorca, an elegant, historic city sprawled beneath the ruins of a 13th-century fortress, is justly celebrated throughout Spain for its wealth of magnificent Baroque architecture. Its elegant avenues and squares are scattered with sumptuous escutcheoned mansions and lavish churches. The beautiful Plaza de España at the heart of the old quarter is overlooked by the splendid Ex-Colegiata de San Patricio *(see p52)* and the arcaded 17th-century town hall. A clutch of museums is dedicated to Lorca's lengthy history and ancient traditions, including the Holy Week processions for which it is famous. *Map K4*

9 Aledo

The peaceful medieval village of Aledo is huddled tightly behind vestiges of ancient walls, on a rocky outcrop that juts out alarmingly over the surrounding valley. Perched at the tip of the village is a watchtower, surrounded by a modern walkway offering beautiful views over the terraced hillsides and distant peaks. Three km (2 miles) away, an elegant 18th-century sanctuary with a richly carved *artesonado* ceiling houses a much-venerated image of the local patron saint, Santa Eulalia. Aledo sits on the borders of the wonderful Regional Park of the Sierra de Espuña. *Map L4*

10 Sierra de Espuña

A lush and verdant stretch of forested mountains in the heart of Murcia has been converted into the spectacular Regional Park of the Sierra de Espuña *(see pp20–21)*, a paradise for hikers, bird-watchers and anyone seeking respite from the searing summer heat. In spring, the slopes are covered with a carpet of wild flowers, and there's a network of excellent walking trails adapted to hikers of all abilities. Wild boar, rare squirrels and mountain sheep have made the forests their home.

Sierra de Espuña, view from park entrance

A Day in Inland Murcia

Morning

Allow a full day for this drive, which includes time for hiking. Begin at the little mountain village of **Aledo**, with panoramic views of peaks and valleys, before following the signs for Bullas and turning off at the **Sierra de Espuña Regional Park**. Continue along the twisting mountain road, which offers breathtaking glimpses of forested crags. The left-hand turn signposted *pozos de nieve* will take you to the snow wells, reached by a path from the small car park at the crook of the road. This is a great place for a hike and a picnic. Return to the Collado Bermejo and take the right-hand fork through forests and glades of wild flowers to the **visitor information centre** and exhibition.

Have lunch at the nearby **Fuente del Hilo**, where wild boar snuffle fearlessly at the doorway for dropped crumbs.

Afternoon

Next, take the signposted road for the little hamlet of El Berro, close to the arid wilderness of the **Barrancos de Gebas**, otherwise known as the "Bad Lands". There are panoramic views from the **Caserío de Gebas** on the C3315. The road leads north to Pliego, a sleepy village topped with a ruined tower, and on to **Mula** *(see p47)*, with its fascinating medieval centre and striking ruined castle. Join the locals for an old-fashioned country dinner at the **Venta La Magdalena** *(see p109)*.

Left **El Centro de Artesanía** Right **Carlos at work in his Confitería Carlos**

Top 10 Murcia City Shops

1 El Centro de Artesanía
The best place to find all kinds of Murcian arts and crafts, from ceramics to handmade figurines. It's run by the Murcian provincial government, and there's another branch in Lorca. *C/Francisco Rabal 8 • Map S4 • 968 28 45 64*

2 Artesanía Abellán
Murcia is famous for its beautifully crafted *belenes*, the figures used to decorate traditional nativity scenes at Christmas. This old-fashioned shop, just outside Murcia, sells a host of figures, from angels and saints to farmers and fishermen. *C/Mayor 16, Puente Tocinos • Map N3*

3 Confitería Carlos
The Arabs introduced the delicious pastries for which Murcia is still celebrated. The tempting selection in this cake shop includes *paparajotes*, light, lemon-flavoured pastries. *C/Jaime I El Conquistador 7 • Map T4 • 968 23 30 20*

4 Manuel Nicolás Almansa
There are more weird and wonderful nativity figurines at this traditional workshop. *C/Belenes 12 • Map N3*

5 Enoteca Selección Casa Rambla
There's a huge selection of local, Spanish and international wines at this enormous shop, along with a good range of liqueurs and fiery local spirits. *C/Saavedra Fajardo 15 • Map U5 • 968 35 56 51*

6 La Tienda de Paparajote
This little souvenir shop close to Murcia's biggest sight, the extravagantly Baroque cathedral *(see pp28–9)*, sells all kinds of gifts, from t-shirts to hard-to-find local delicacies such as handmade sweets from inland villages. *C/Apóstoles 14 • Map U6 • 968 93 13 56*

7 Confitería Viena
Located in one of Murcia's pedestrianized streets behind the cathedral, this bakery sells all types of traditional cakes and desserts. *C/Trapería 30 • Map U5 • 968 21 18 00*

8 Mercado de las Verónicas
Set in a whimsical Modernista building, Murcia's delightful covered market offers a huge variety of fresh produce, including fish and locally reared meats. *Plano de San Francisco • Map T6*

9 Carrusel
This shop offers a vast range of souvenirs and gifts, as well as jewellery, handbags and clothes. *C/Trapería 25 • Map U5 • 968 22 18 13*

10 Bonache
If you are planning a picnic, stop off at this bakery for some *pasteles de carne* or *empanadas*, traditional pastries stuffed with all kinds of fillings from tuna to ham. There's also a vegetarian version made with *pisto* (like ratatouille). *Plaza Flores 8 • Map T6 • 968 21 20 83*

Price Categories

For a three course meal for one with half a bottle of wine (or equivalent meal), taxes and extra charges.

€	under €20
€€	€20–€30
€€€	€30–€40
€€€€	€40–€50
€€€€€	over €50

La Tapa

Top 10 Murcia City Tapas Bars

1 La Muralla

This smart pub located in Murcia's fanciest hotel *(see p126)* is an inviting place to drink and is well-known for the stretch of Arabic wall incorporated into its design. *C/Apóstoles 34 • Map U6 • 968 21 22 39 • Open 4pm daily • €€*

2 El Arco

This elegant café-bar has a huge terrace out on a graceful square, perfect for lingering over breakfast or a light lunch, even better for people-watching in the evenings. *C/Arco de Santo Domingo s/n • Map U5 • 968 21 97 67 • €*

3 La Tapa

A simple, buzzy tapas bar on one of Murcia's liveliest squares. There's plenty of choice, and you can sit out on the terrace to watch the action. *Plaza de las Flores 13 • Map T5 • 968 21 13 17 • €*

4 Pacopepe

The tapas at Pacopepe are among the best in town. Try the delicious stuffed artichokes, or one of the celebrated mushroom dishes – everything is fresh from the orchards and gardens around the city. *C/Madre de Dios 14 • Map T6 • 968 21 95 87 • Closed Sun • €€*

5 Heladería Chambi

Stop off for a refreshing ice cream or an ice-cold *granizado* (crushed ice drink), which you can take away or consume on the tiny street terrace. *Avda Alfonso X El Sabio 2 • Map U5 • €*

6 Cafetín Árabe Abu Nuwas

Sink into the cushions at this magical Arabic-style tearoom and bar, where you can choose from more than 150 different infusions – plus wonderful Moroccan pastries. *C/Ruipérez 8 • Map T5 • 968 22 20 42 • Opens 4pm daily • €*

7 Los Zagales

Just around the corner from the cathedral, this is a great place to share a plate of tapas either with friends or with the locals. *C/Polo de Medina 4 • Map U6 • 968 21 55 79 • Closed Sun • €*

8 Pequeña Taberna Típica

The name says it all. This typical tavern serves great Murcian specialities, with first-rate local cured sausages and hams. *Plaza San Juan • Map U6 • 968 21 98 40 • Closed Mon in winter, Sun in summer • €€*

9 El Ahorcado Feliz

The "Happy Hanged Man" is the most unusual café in Murcia. The furniture is made up of flea-market finds; the floor is a mosaic of smashed plates and ceramics. Great for a coffee, even better for a drink. *C/Cánovas del Castillo 35 • Map V6 • No tel • Open 3pm daily • €*

10 Jota Ele

Another local favourite, Jota Ele has excellent old-fashioned tapas, including delicious local hams and conserves, as well as smoked fish. *Plaza Santa Isabel 3 • Map T5 • 968 22 07 30 • Closed Sun • €€*

Left **Embutidos at Matanza** Right **Semana Santa procession**

Top 10 Local Traditions and Festivals

1 Matanza
As in olden times, farming families in inland towns still slaughter their pigs every November to create the famous *embutidos* (cured sausages and hams) *(see p64)*.

2 Semana Santa
Holy Week is a huge event, with lavish processions taking place throughout the week. The most spectacular are held in Murcia City, Cartagena, Jumilla, Lorca and Cieza.

3 Martes Santo
On Holy Tuesday, an ear-splitting parade of drummers processes through Mula during the *Gran Tamborada*. There are other *tamboradas* at Moratalla on Maundy Thursday and Good Friday. *Map L2 (Mula), K1 (Moratalla)*

4 Viernes Santo
Good Friday has a special significance in Murcia City. The week's processions culminate with a parade of gilded *pasos* (floats) featuring sculptures by the Baroque artist Francisco Salzillo *(see p31)*. *Map N3*

5 Fiestas de Primavera
Murcia City's Spring Fiesta (from the Tuesday after Easter Sunday) begins with the Battle of the Flowers and the *Bando de la Huerta*, a parade of amusing satirical floats. A pagan ritual called the "Burial of the Sardine" marks the end of the fiesta. *Map N3*

6 Fiestas de la Cruz de Caravaca
In the first week of May, Caravaca commemorates ancient legends and miracles with processions of "knights" on horseback and other traditional events in the Festival of the Cross of Caravaca *(see pp 46, 51)*. *Map K2*

7 Carnavales
Carnival is an excuse to party hard across the region *(see p50)*. Águilas really goes to town as parades process riotously through the streets and parties erupt in every bar and square. *Map L6*

8 Fiesta de Cartagineses y Romanos
Mock battles between Moors and Christians are common in the Costa Blanca. In Cartagena's Festival of the Carthaginians and the Romans, held in September, they commemorate the battles and victory of the Romans over the city. *Map P5*

9 Fiesta de la Vendimia
Jumilla celebrates its ancient Wine Harvest Festival in the last two weeks of August. *Map A4*

10 Festival Internacional de Teatro, Música y Danza
One of the biggest cultural events on the Murcian summer calendar, San Javier's International Festival of Theatre, Music and Dance is a great opportunity to see international performers at venues across the city. *Map N3*

Rincón de Pepe

Price Categories

For a three course meal for one with half a bottle of wine (or equivalent meal), taxes and extra charges.

€	under €20
€€	€20–€30
€€€	€30–€40
€€€€	€40–€50
€€€€€	over €50

TOP 10 Places to Eat

1 Cándido, Lorca

This local favourite specializes in mountain stews made with beans and flavoured with cured meat. *C/Santo Domingo 13 • Map K4 • 968 46 69 07 • Closed Sun D • €€*

2 Rincón de Paco, Caravaca de la Cruz

Bullfighting posters and other taurine memorabilia line the bar at this popular local eatery. *C/Lonjas 5 • Map K2 • 968 70 83 90 • Closed Tue • €€*

3 Charco Ontur, Jumilla

A carnivore's delight, this friendly local restaurant specializes in succulent meats such as kid and lamb, simply grilled over charcoal. *C/Barón del Solar 76 • Map A4 • Closed Mon D, Tue • €€*

4 El Teatro, Lorca

Ceramic tiles and sturdy wooden furniture set the scene at this down-to-earth restaurant, which serves good local dishes like *pan de Calatrava*, a home-made custard-like dessert. *Plaza de Colón 12 • Map K4 • 968 46 99 09 • Closed Sun D, Mon, Aug • €€*

5 El Chaleco, Alhama de Murcia

At this family-run restaurant you can dine on traditional Murcian specialities, wonderful home-made desserts and a good selection of regional wines. *Avenida Bastarreche 9 • Map M3 • 968 63 01 04 • Closed Mon, Sun D (Jul, Aug), 1st half Aug • €€€*

6 Venta La Magdalena, Baños de Mula

Locals love the old-fashioned home cooking at this big roadside eatery, including a special rice dish made with snails and rabbit. *Ctra de Murcia Km 17 • Map M2 • 968 66 05 68 • Closed Wed, mid-Jul–mid-Aug • €€*

7 Las Cadenas, Murcia

This relaxed local restaurant serves Murcian dishes featuring meat, seafood and other fresh produce, but the highlight here is the home-made desserts. *C/ Apóstoles 10, Murcia • Map U6 • 968 22 09 24 • Closed Sun • €€*

8 Rincón de Pepe, Murcia

This handsome, formal restaurant in Murcia's best hotel offers elaborate regional dishes accompanied by an excellent wine list *(see p67)*.

9 Hispano II, Murcia

This hotel-restaurant in the heart of the city serves fresh Mediterreanean cuisine based on whatever is most appetizing in the market that day. *C/Radio Murcia 3 • Map U5 • 968 21 61 52 • Closed Sun D in Jul & Aug • €€€*

10 El Sol, Cehegín

This old-fashioned restaurant in the heart of medieval Cehegín serves traditional Murcian dishes with a creative twist. You can dine out on a little terrace. *C/ Mayor 17 • Map K2 • 968 74 00 64 • Closed Mon, 1st half July • €€*

Remember that most restaurants – even the more expensive ones – have very reasonably priced lunchtime menús del día.

STREETSMART

Left **Tourist office** Middle **Information sign in Alicante** Right **Wheelchair access to the beach**

TOP 10 Planning Your Trip

1 Climate and When to Go

Winter is mild, summer hot and dry. Spring and early autumn find the country at its lushest, and there's room on the beach. In summer, it's crowded and more expensive, but good for the hedonistic nightlife.

2 Visas and Red Tape

EU citizens and those from countries within the Shengen Agreement can enter Spain with a valid ID card or passport. Americans, Canadians, Australians and New Zealanders can stay with no visa for up to 90 days. Citizens of other countries may require a visa.

3 Embassies and Consulates

These provide information about visiting, working in and retiring to Spain, and have useful websites.

4 Tourist Offices

The slick and efficient Spanish National Tourism Service provides a wealth of glossy brochures, maps and leaflets; their website is a useful starting point.
www.spain.info

5 Resources for Disabled Travellers

Facilities are generally inadequate, but have improved dramatically in recent years. The following organizations can give you general information in advance.
UK *Holiday Care Information Unit: 0845 124 9971. www.holidaycare.org.uk* • ***USA*** *SATH: 212 447 7284. www.sath.org*

6 Languages

Valencian (related to Catalan) and Spanish (Castilian) are the two official languages of the Autonomous Community of Valencia, of which the Costa Blanca is part. Spanish is spoken in Murcia. Valencian is more common inland, particularly in the northern Costa Blanca.

7 Internet Sources

There are several excellent multilingual websites dedicated to the Costa Blanca. See the Directory for a list.

8 Insurance

EU citizens get state health care on production of an E111 form (bring this from your own country), but it's a complicated process, and private travel insurance is highly recommended. The same applies to non-EU visitors. Dentistry is not covered under such agreements, and can be expensive.

9 What to Take

Casual dress is acceptable, but bring a smart outfit for upmarket restaurants or clubs. Evenings inland can get cool, so bring a light sweater. Sunscreen is essential and mosquito repellent useful. You'll need sturdy footwear in the regional parks if you are planning to do some hiking. It's handy too to have a plug adaptor.

10 Public Holidays

On public holidays, some bars and restaurants and most shops will be closed, especially in the inland regions. The transport system runs restricted services, and if you are planning to do any travelling, you should book tickets well in advance. If the holiday falls midweek, it's common to take an extra day off, forming a long weekend known as a *puente* (bridge).

Directory

Main Tourist Offices

Alicante: Rambla de Méndez Núñez 23 • 965 20 00 00

Murcia City: Plz. Cardenal Belluga, Edif. Ayuntamiento • 968 35 87 49

Spanish National Tourist Offices

UK: 79 New Cavendish Street, London W1W 6XB • 020 7317 2010

USA: 666 Fifth Avenue, New York NY 10103 • 212 265 8822

Useful Websites

www.costablanca.org • www.alicanteturismo.com • www.murciaciudad.com • www.comunidad-valenciana.com • www.carm.es

Preceding pages **A street in Alicante's Barrio de Santa Cruz**

Left **Eurolines coach ticket office** Right **A train on the national RENFE network**

Top 10 Getting There

1 Flying Europe to Alicante (Alacant)

Alicante is served by numerous "no-frills" carriers including Ryanair, EasyJet and Spanair, as well as by major airlines from other Spanish and European cities. Book early in high season and check the Internet for the best deals.

2 Flying North America to Alicante

There are no direct flights. US and Canadian visitors usually have to change at Madrid, Barcelona or elsewhere. Delta Airlines fly to Barcelona, from where you can take the high-speed Euromed train to Alicante. Iberia serves most major North American airports.

3 Flying Europe to Murcia

There are direct flights from the UK, Ireland and (usually via Madrid) most major European cities. In high season charter flights can offer great deals.

4 Flying North America to Murcia

There are no direct flights from North America to Murcia. Try Iberia to Madrid, plus an onward connection, or British Airways via London.

5 Ferries from the Balearics

Denia (Dénia) is the main Costa Blanca ferry port for the Balearics. Both Balearia and Iscomar run regular car and passenger ferries from Ibiza and Palma (Mallorca).

6 Trains

Spain's national rail system, RENFE, is clean, efficient and inexpensive. The plush, high-speed Euromed service connects major towns between Barcelona, Alicante and Murcia; overnight services run from Paris to Madrid and Barcelona. Book in advance. *www.renfe.es*

7 Coaches

International coach services run to Alicante, Benidorm, Murcia and most larger resorts in summer. Coaches are cheap, but journeys are long (London to Alicante, for example, takes at least 26 hours). Try Eurolines for starters. *www.eurolines.com*

8 Roads

The main motorway down Spain's east coast is the AP7 (aka E15); the tolls can be quite dear. The toll-free N332 road links Valencia and Murcia, but gets very busy in high season.

9 Package Holidays

Countless tour operators offer package deals to the Costa Blanca, ranging from self-catering apartments to smart hotels. They are inexpensive, but focus on the biggest, most crowded resorts.

10 Sailing

Sailing is enormously popular all along the Costa Blanca. Virtually every resort boasts a well-equipped marina, including Alicante, Denia, Xabia, Teulada, Calp, Altea, Benidorm, La Vila Joiosa, Santa Pola, the Isla Tabarca, Torrevieja, Santiago de la Ribera, Cartagena, Cabo de Palos, Puerto de Mazarrón, and Águilas. The Alicante port authority is a useful source of information. *www.puertoalicante.com*

Directory

Airports

Alicante airport: El Altet
• 902 40 47 04
• www.aena.es

Airlines

Aer Lingus (Ireland)
• (353) 818 365 044
• www.aerlingus.com

Air Canada
• (888) 247 2262
• www.aircanada.com

American Airlines (USA)
• (800) 433 7300
• www.aa.com

British Airways (UK)
• 0844 493 0787 • www.britishairways.com

British Midland/bmi (UK)
• 0870 607 0555
• www.flybmi.com

Iberia • 0870 609 0500 (UK); 1800 772 4642 (USA) • www.iberia.com

EasyJet (UK)
• 0905 821 0905
• www.easyjet.com

For tips on travel within the Costa Blanca region **See p114**

Left **The narrow-gauge 'Trenet'** Middle **Local buses** Right **Taxis**

TOP 10 Getting Around

1 By Road

A car is often a nuisance rather than a benefit in the larger towns and resorts, which are always clogged with traffic, particularly during the evening rush hour (6–8pm). Parking can be a problem, but larger towns have underground car parks which charge around €5–€10 per day. Your own transport is virtually essential to see the remoter corners of the Costa Blanca.

2 Rules of the Road

Speed limits are 120 kph on motorways *(autopistas* and *autovías)*, 100 kph on main roads, and 50 kph in built-up areas. Seat belts are compulsory in the front seats, and in the rear where fitted. The legal alcohol limit is 0.25 mg/l; this is regularly flouted, but anyone caught can be fined up to €300 on the spot.

3 Car Rental

There are car hire offices at the airports, and plenty more at train stations and in major towns and resorts. The cheapest deals can usually be found over the Internet; many airlines offer concessions. It's advisable to book well in advance during holiday periods. *www.alicante-travel-car.com • www.avis.es • www.easycar.com • www.holidayautos.co.uk • www.iberocar.com*

4 Train

The rail network offers a bewildering array of services. The most useful on the Costa Blanca are the local *(cercanías)* and regional *(regionales)* trains which connect some larger cities and resorts. They are generally punctual and inexpensive.

5 El Trenet

A narrow-gauge train runs from El Campello (on the outskirts of Alicante and connected to the city centre by tram) to Denia (Dénia), stopping at most resorts. It is scenic, especially between Altea and Denia, but very slow.

6 FEVE

The FEVE train station in Cartagena is the starting point for the narrow-gauge railway that links the city with the small resort of Los Nietos on the Mar Menor. It's not a very scenic route, but it's cheap and convenient.

7 Local Buses and Coaches

Local bus services are rarely useful for visitors as most sights are in the town centres. But many inland villages are not on the train network, and are only accessible by bus. Different companies serve different areas, which can be confusing, but there are information offices in bus stations, and the tourist offices also have timetables.

Alicante bus/coach station: C/Portugal 17. Map T3. 965 13 07 00 • Murcia bus/coach station: C/San Andrés s/n. Map S5. 968 29 22 11

8 Taxis

Taxis are cheap and plentiful – at least in the larger towns and resorts. They can be hailed on the street or from taxi stands; a green light on the top indicates that they are free. Otherwise, you can, of course, call for a taxi *(see below)*. *Radio Taxi: 965 25 25 11 (Alicante); 968 24 88 00 (Murcia)* • ***Wheelchair-accessible taxis*** *Radio Taxi: 965 86 18 18 (Benidorm); 620 99 00 33 (Murcia)*

9 Cycling

Competitive cycling is very popular in Spain *(see p44)*. Pottering around the countryside on a bike is less common, but nonetheless delightful. Bike hire is common in resorts and at rural hotels.

10 On Foot

All the towns and villages are best explored on foot. The main sights are usually clustered in the historic centres, and a stroll will throw up all kinds of delightful details that you might otherwise miss. Hikers are spoilt for choice; there are several Natural and Regional Parks, as well as long-distance walking trails, such as the GR7 and the GR92.

Note: *Disabled travellers should book taxis 24 hours ahead.*

A pharmacy – first port of call for minor ailments

TOP 10 Health and Security

1 Emergency Numbers

In an emergency dial 112. English-speaking operators will connect you to the appropriate service. There are also free direct numbers for police, ambulance and fire brigade *(see Directory)*.

2 Police

Spain has several types of police. The *Policía Nacional* (brown uniforms) deal with urban crime, so report anything stolen to them. The *Policía Local* (in dark blue) deal with minor urban crime and traffic control. The *Guardia Civil* (green uniforms) police the main highways and rural areas. Police stations are listed in phone books under *Comisarías*.

3 Health Issues

No inoculations are needed for Spain. Beware mainly of heatstroke and sunburn. Use sunscreen, wear a hat, and stay in the shade between noon and 4pm. Jellyfish stings are an occasional nuisance. Rinse them in fresh water with bicarbonate of soda.

4 Prescriptions

Bring any prescription drugs you require with you in your hand baggage. Spanish medication may differ from your own in name, dosage and form, so you should bring the generic (rather than brand) name of your medicine in case you need a repeat prescription.

5 Pharmacies

Spanish pharmacists are highly trained and very useful for minor ailments. Most major cities have at least one 24-hour pharmacy *(farmacia)*. Its details are posted in all pharmacy windows.

6 Multilingual Doctors

The Costa Blanca has a huge expat community, with doctors and dentists catering to all nationalities. Hotels and pharmacies can advise you, and the English-language paper *Costa Blanca News* carries ads. If you're using the EU reciprocal healthcare agreement, make sure the doctor belongs to the Spanish healthcare system.

7 Women Travellers

Women travellers face no difficulties on the cosmopolitan Costa, besides a little flirtation and a few wolf whistles. Dress modestly in the inland towns to ward off unwanted attention, but in big towns and resorts virtually anything goes.

8 Disabled Travellers

Facilities are slowly improving for disabled travellers. Tourist offices provide details of wheelchair-accessible hotels, beaches and sights, and restaurants usually do their best, but it is wise to call in advance. Some city buses are adapted for wheelchairs, and there are special taxi services *(see p114)*.

9 Petty Crime

Petty crime is fairly common, particularly in high season. Lock valuables in a hotel safety deposit box; keep a copy of your passport (separately). Don't leave valuables in your car, and open the glove compartment to show there is nothing to steal. Wear a bag that straps across you, and be wary of "helpful" strangers.

10 Serious Crime

Serious crime is comparatively rare on the Costa Blanca. But in the cities it's wise to avoid wandering around unlit streets in the seedier neighbourhoods.

Directory

Emergency Numbers
112 (general)
092 (local police)
091 (national police)
080 (fire brigade)
965 25 25 25 (Red Cross)
965 14 40 00 (paramedics)

Major Hospitals
Alicante: C/Maestro Alonso 109 • 965 93 83 00

Benidorm: Dr. Ramón y Cajal 7 • 966 87 87 97

Murcia: Avda Marqués de los Vélez s/n • 968 36 09 00

For further advice on personal security **See p117**

Left **Withdrawing cash at an ATM** Middle **A typical payphone** Right **International newspapers**

Top 10 Banking and Communications

1 Currency

Spain's national currency is the euro, which is divided into 100 *céntimos*. Although all prices are marked in euros, people still often talk in *pesetas* for larger items such as houses and cars.

2 Changing Money

There are money-changing facilities at the airport, and almost all banks offer exchange services. The outlets clustered in the resorts often charge a hefty commission. Banks are usually open 8:30am–2pm Mon–Fri, but in the larger towns some open on Saturday mornings.

3 ATMs

Cash machines can be found on almost every street corner, even in the smallest towns. Look for a sign saying "*Telebanco*" Instructions are posted in a variety of languages. Spanish banks don't charge a commission for using ATMs, but check whether your own bank will charge you.

4 Credit Cards

Credit cards are commonly accepted in shops, larger hotels and big restaurants, though less so in smaller towns and villages. They are accepted at train stations but almost never at sights and monuments, so ensure that you have enough cash with you.

5 Traveller's Cheques

Traveller's cheques are a useful safety precaution since they can be replaced if lost or stolen. Bring cheques in euros to avoid paying commission. Note that they are rarely accepted as a mode of payment, except in the larger hotels and resorts.

6 Post Offices and *Estancos*

Post offices are identified by a yellow sign saying *Correos y Telégrafos*. Larger branches offer fax, telegram, poste restante and mail-box services. *Estancos* (newspaper kiosks) and tobacco shops sell stamps. Post offices are also located in some El Corte Inglés shops.

7 Phones

Public phone booths are blue or green and very common. Most take phonecards (€5, €10 and €20 from *estancos* – *see above*) and some accept credit cards. Phones provided in hotel rooms can be very dear. Most foreign mobiles will work in Spain, but it's advisable to check with your service provider in advance.

8 Internet

Internet cafés are easy to find, and tourist information offices have lists of them. Few will allow you to plug in your laptop, but many larger hotels provide modem points in the bedrooms or WiFi areas.

9 Newspapers and Magazines

The main Spanish national broadsheets are *El País* (left-leaning) and *El Mundo* (right-leaning). The long-established *Costa Blanca News* is a weekly English-language paper dedicated to the enormous expat community. International press is easily available in Alicante, Murcia City and all the resorts.

10 TV and Radio

TV is a constant presence in most bars, and a set comes as standard even in *pensiones*. Radio fans tune into RNE1 (88.2FM: news/current affairs), Radio Clásica (96.5FM: classical music), Radio 3 (93.2FM: pop), or the BBC World Service (98.5FM).

Directory

Main Post Offices
Alicante: C/Alemania 7
Murcia: Plaza Circular s/n
• www.correos.es

International Codes
Dial 00 + country code (USA and Canada 1; UK 44) + area code + local number.

Directory Enquiries
National: 11822
International: 11818

Lost Credit Cards
American Express: 902 37 56 37
Diner's Club: 902 40 11 12
MC/Visa: 900 99 11 24

August on the Costa Blanca

Top 10 Things to Avoid

1 Gambling Games

You are bound at some point to come across this scene: a gaggle of people clustered round a makeshift table in the street, someone expertly flipping three little cups, one of which apparently contains a counter. If you're asked to guess the right cup, beware. This is an old gambling scam, and there are never any winners!

2 "Helpful" Strangers

Watch out for these on the street or at petrol stations. They usually work in pairs. While one is telling you that you've dropped your keys or pretends to brush some dirt from your shoulder, the other is relieving you of your wallet.

3 Eating Dinner at 7pm

Along the coast you can find a meal at any time you like. But in the rural inland regions, you will have to adapt to Spanish time and aim to eat around 9pm – unless you want to dine alone. Note too that many restaurants are closed on Sunday evenings.

4 Visiting Museums on Mondays

Almost all the museums in the Costa Blanca are closed on Mondays, so plan your days out accordingly. Churches, however, are usually open, as are all the Regional and Natural Parks. Monday's also a good shopping day.

5 Conducting Business at Siesta Time

The traditional Spanish siesta may be going out of style, but there is still a long break in the afternoons for most shops and offices, as well as smaller museums and monuments. Banks are closed in the afternoon, and most post offices close for several hours over lunchtime. Churches also regularly close between 1pm and 3pm (often for longer), so get your sightseeing done early.

6 Buying Fish on Mondays

Trawlers don't work on Sundays and Mondays. As a result, the fish section of most covered markets will be closed on Monday. Whether you are buying fish to cook yourself or choosing it from a restaurant menu, it is unlikely to be particularly fresh, and should be avoided.

7 August on the Costa Blanca

August is the traditional holiday month in Spain, when shops, offices, restaurants and hotels across the country close down, and families pile down to the coast. As a result, accommodation on the Costa Blanca is always dearer and harder to find in August, while the beaches can be unpleasantly crowded, and the roads clogged with an endless stream of traffic.

8 Discarding a Lit Cigarette

The dry, scrubby slopes of the inland regions are at their most fragile during the searing heat of July and August. Discarded cigarettes are a major cause of forest fires and environmental damage. Take care throughout the region.

9 Taking Valuables to the Beach

While the Costa Blanca is relatively safe, petty crime is not uncommon. Taking your valuables to the beach is asking for trouble. Ask your hotel to lock them in a safety deposit box, and only take a small amount of cash with you, particularly if your belongings are likely to be unattended while you're in the water.

10 Wasting Water

Water shortages can be a problem in the Costa Blanca during July and August, when demand is greatest. They are unlikely to affect visitors, particularly in the smartest hotels, but you may be asked to take care with the water supply in inland regions.

For more health tips See p115

Left **Golfing in Alicante** Right **Fishing at Torrevieja**

TOP 10 Specialist Tours

1 Aspects of Spain
This company offers self-catering villa holidays to suit all budgets in the northern Costa Blanca region (mainly around Xàbia (Jávea), Calp (Calpe) and Altea. *Alma Place, Belmont St, Bognor Regis PO21 1LY • (01243) 888 114 • www.aspectsofspain.com*

2 Bill Goff Golf Tours
Tailor-made golf packages to the La Manga resort on the Mar Menor. This is a family-oriented resort with a huge array of sports facilities. *Unit 9, Bankside, The Watermark, Gateshead NE11 9SY • 0800 915 1804 • www.billgoff.com*

3 Erna Low Body and Soul
Indulge yourself! Erna Low offer spa holidays in luxurious surroundings at their hotels in Alicante (Alacant) and Denia (Dénia), and soon on the Mar Menor. They can also arrange combined golf–spa breaks. *9 Reece Mews, London SW7 3HE • (020) 7594 0290 • www.bodyandsoulholidays.com*

4 Exodus Travel
Exodus offer a range of holidays including rock-climbing, walking, cycling – just about any sport you care to try. *Grangemills, Weir Rd, London SW12 OME • (020) 8675 5550 • www.exodus.co.uk*

5 Headwater Holidays
Headwater run guided walking holidays on the northern Costa Blanca for travellers of moderate fitness. Hikers average 14 km (9 miles) a day through the spectacular scenery of the Sierra de Serrella. Accommodation at traditional family-run inns is included. *The Old School House, Chester Road, Northwich CW8 1LE • (01606) 720 033 • www.headwater.com*

6 Direct Connection
This tour operator offers a wide variety of villas, apartments and hotels along the Costa Blanca, as well as flights. Check the company website for special deals and late availability. *Harvest House, Lynderswood Farm, Lynderswood Lane, London Road, Braintree, Essex • 0845 123 2523 • holidays@directconnection.co.uk • www.directconnection.co.uk/blanca/*

7 Costa del Carping
If you want to try your hand at fishing, this company offers everything from tailor-made packages to one-day fishing trips. Costa del Carping will take you to the best locations for catching carp, barbel and catfish. They will also provide you with fishing permits, insurance, tackle, bait and lunch. *637 93 96 80 • www.costadelcarping.com*

8 VacationRentals.com
Surprisingly few US-based tour operators offer holidays to the Costa Blanca. VacationRentals.com is one, arranging flights, accommodation, car hire and a variety of other services. *3801 S Capital of Texas Highway, Suite 150, Austin, TX 78704 • www.vacationrentals.com*

9 Comtours
This US operator runs fully escorted coach tours of Andalucía and the Costa Blanca region lasting seven or nine days. Holidays include flights, accommodation and the services of a multilingual guide. *1290 Bassett Road, Cleveland, OH 44145 • (440) 835 1480 or 1-800 248 1331 (toll-free) • www.comtours.com*

10 Ciclo Costa Blanca
This local company provides self-catering accommodation and hotel-based training camps for cyclists, plus detailed route maps ranging from simple, flat tours around Denia to tough mountain climbs. They can arrange for rides with local clubs, and competitive cyclists can even take part in sportives. *C/Bacalla 29, Denia • Map H2 • 965 78 01 32 • www.ciclocostablanca.com*

Left **Children's clothes in a store** Right **Terra Mítica, near Benidorm**

TOP 10 Tips for Families

1 Attitudes to Children

The Spanish adore children, and yours will be indulged wherever they go. Children are treated like small adults, and it's not unusual to see them out in restaurants with their parents late at night, or playing outside a café while their families chat away. There are plenty of outdoor playgrounds in every town and resort.

2 Accommodation

Almost all hotels welcome children. Family rooms are common, and some hotels will allow children to stay in their parents' room at no extra charge. Perhaps the most convenient (and cost-effective) way to travel as a family is to rent an apartment or a *casa rural*.

3 Hotel Programmes

Some of the larger hotels offer a programme of activities for guests of all ages, including anything from swimming lessons to organized games and coach excursions.

4 Babysitting

Babysitters are generally available in larger hotels (24 hours' notice usually required); much less so in smaller hotels and *pensiones*. A few hotels have day-care facilities, so check in advance. Larger cities have drop-in children's centres with play areas and cafés, but parents usually have to stay.

5 Family Meals

Most restaurants are happy to cater for children, though few offer a dedicated children's menu. They are usually more than happy to provide a small portion, or to offer something simple that might not be on the menu. High chairs are not common. Call your chosen restaurant in advance to see if they can provide one.

6 Shopping for Children

There are scores of children's clothes and toy shops in the larger towns. Nappies and formula milk can be found in supermarkets and pharmacies. Make sure you stock up for weekends, as very few shops open on Sundays.

7 Family-oriented Attractions

There's no shortage of family attractions, with the enormous theme park Terra Mítica near Benidorm, plus water-parks, safari parks and fun-parks right across the region. Many horse-riding centres offer pony treks for children, and sailing centres, notably around the Mar Menor, offer classes for beginners of all ages. The Natural and Regional Parks have hiking trails to suit all levels.

8 Child-friendly Beaches

The main resort beaches are very well-geared toward children, with play areas right on the beach, as well as showers, toilets and snack bars to keep everyone happy. There are usually lifeguard posts and a medical tent in case of mishap. If visiting the quieter coves, find out what the swimming conditions are before venturing into the sea.

9 Attractions for Teenagers

If the beaches begin to pall, teenagers can shop till they drop, visit the theme parks and water-parks, or indulge in every imaginable sporting activity. Some museums are great for teenagers, including Alicante's hi-tech archaeology museum MARQ *(see p12)* and Murcia City's Museo Hidráulico *(see 30)*.

10 Nightlife

The party scene is wild during the summer, and older teenagers can take their pick of dozens of nightclubs and bars. The best are the *terrazas*, usually open only during the summer months and with big outdoor dance floors. The more infamous Benidorm bars, with their serious drinking culture and resultant brawling, are best avoided.

Left **Tipping** Right **Leisurely café lunch**

Top 10 Eating and Drinking Tips

1 Breakfast

Breakfast in Spain is traditionally a light and hurried affair – perhaps a pastry or a croissant washed down with milky coffee *(café con leche)*. Full English breakfast – complete with egg, bacon and sausage – is available at countless expat-run cafés in the major resorts. Most hotels offer a buffet-style breakfast which will accommodate visitors of all nationalities.

2 Lunch

Lunch, usually eaten around 2pm, is often the major meal of the day. It tends to consist of two or three courses with a glass or two of wine. The Spanish like to take their time over lunch; most smaller shops and local businesses will close for at least two hours. Sunday lunch is often a big family affair, and can last well into the evening.

3 Dinner

The Spanish don't usually sit down to dinner before around 9pm. The vast numbers of foreign visitors are catered for with earlier dining hours in all the coastal resorts. Evening meals tend to be lighter than lunches. Eating out at weekends is very popular, so it is always wise to book ahead. The Spanish plug the gap between lunch and late dinner with a few tapas at a local bar.

4 The Tapeo

The *tapeo*, a kind of bar crawl from tapas bar to tapas bar, is an institution in Alicante (Alacant) and in Murcia City. Both cities boast dozens of tapas bars, many of them famous for a particular speciality: for instance, especially good ham, or delicious home-made *croquetas* (potato croquettes). If you want a larger portion, ask for a *ración*.

5 Vegetarians

Vegetarians have a hard time in Spain, where even apparently innocuous vegetable dishes are regularly flavoured with ham or *chorizo* (cured sausage). There are few vegetarian restaurants, but most places will make up something simple, particularly when given notice. Otherwise, reliable stand-bys include *tortilla* (potato omelette) and platters of Spanish cheese. Salads usually feature tinned tuna *(atún)*; ask them to leave out any ingredients that you don't want.

6 Tipping

Spaniards usually just leave a few small coins on the bar when having a drink or a coffee, and round up the bill when in restaurants. Most foreign visitors leave a tip of around 10 per cent at restaurants, particularly in the resorts.

7 Getting Drunk

While plenty of foreigners come to Spain for the cheap booze, getting drunk is generally frowned upon. There is a huge drinking culture in some of the resorts, fuelled by packs of young northern European holiday-makers intent on having such a good time they can't remember it, but the Spanish tend to drink only moderately, and generally accompany their drinks with small snacks or tapas.

8 Sunday-night Closing

Be warned that many restaurants, including those in the main resorts, are closed on Sunday or Monday nights.

9 Menú del Día

The fixed-price *menú del día*, served weekday lunchtimes, is geared toward local workers. It usually includes two or three courses with bread and a glass of wine, and is very good value, even at some of the smarter restaurants.

10 Menú de Degustación

Many upmarket restaurants offer a "tasting menu" *(menú de degustación)*, which highlights the restaurant's specialities and changes according to what's freshest. It is generally, though not exclusively, available in the evenings.

Most restaurants will accept major credit cards.

Left **Self-catering apartment** Right **Tucking into the *menú del día***

TOP 10 Budget Tips

1 Low-season Bargains
Flights and hotels are always cheaper out of season, with some fantastic bargains from October to March – particularly if you look around on the Internet. Many of the larger Spanish hotel chains post special deals on their websites during the rest of the year that can make even the smartest four- and five-star hotels surprisingly affordable.

2 Package Deals
Package holidays (the "package" usually includes flights, transfers and accommodation) are big business on the Costa Blanca, with some incredibly low-priced deals. If you don't like the resort, you could use the accommodation provided as your base and spend a few nights somewhere else with the money you save.

3 Pensiones, Hostales and Youth Hostels
Pensiones and *hostales* offer the most basic accommodation and have fewer facilities than hotels, but they are the cheapest places to stay on the Costa Blanca. Many cater to back-packers and families on a budget, and offer triple and quadruple rooms, which bring down the costs even more. There are surprisingly few youth hostels, and many of them are booked up with school parties in the summer months.

4 Self-catering
There are countless self-catering options on the Costa Blanca. These can dramatically bring down costs if you are travelling on a budget. Scores of companies offer apartment or villa rentals. *Casas rurales* (rural houses and apartments) can be spectacularly good value for money for families or large groups.

5 Camping
Campsites are very plentiful on the Costa Blanca, and although prices vary according to facilities and proximity to the beach, they are always pretty cheap. If, however, you have a car, a tent and more than two people, the fees can add up to nearly as much as a cheap hotel room *(see also p131)*.

6 Trains
Of the various train services that run along the Costa Blanca, the luxurious Euromed train is ostensibly the high-speed service, but along this strip of the coast it takes about the same time as the considerably less expensive local and regional trains. The Euromed does have comfortable seats and a café-bar, and even shows films, but it will only save you time if you are taking a long journey, and it will cost at least twice as much as its more lowly rivals.

7 Concessions
Some museums and monuments offer free entry on certain days. Ask at a tourist information office. Students and senior citizens are elegible for concessions at most sites.

8 Family Tickets
Family tickets *(billete familiar)*, usually for two adults and between two and four children, are available at most theme parks and the larger museums, and can offer considerable savings. It's worth asking for one even if it isn't advertised.

9 Picnicking
Picknicking is a delightful way to save money. There are hundreds of wonderful picnic spots *(see pp75 & 87)*, and every town or village has a market where you can pick up fabulous fresh bread, fruit, cheese, ham and pastries for your hamper.

10 Eat at Lunchtime
The fixed-price lunch menu, or *menú del día*, is one of the biggest bargains to be had in Spain. Most restaurants, from the humblest to the glitziest, will offer one. In mid-price establishments this will rarely top €12.

Local buses are good, cheap and clean.

Left **Local crafts** Right **Torrevieja Market**

Top 10 Shopping Tips

1 Opening Hours

Shops are usually open from 10am–2pm and 5–8:30pm Monday to Saturday. Larger shops and department stores are open all day. The big department store El Corte Inglés (which also has a supermarket) is open until 10pm. Very few shops open on Sundays.

2 Customs

Non-EU citizens are permitted to take home one litre of spirits and two litres of wine, as well as 200 cigarettes, 250 grams of tobacco or 50 cigars. EU citizens are limited to "personal use" only, which means in practice that if you turn up at your home airport with more than 10 litres of spirits, 20 litres of fortified wine, 90 litres of wine, 110 litres of beer, 3,200 cigarettes, 200 cigars, 400 cigarillos and 3kg of tobacco, questions are likely to be asked.

3 Fashion

Bargain hunters note: popular international fashion labels originating in Spain (Zara, Mango and Camper, for example) are about a third cheaper in Spain than elsewhere, and there's a wider range of products available.

4 Clothes Sizes

Try everything on; many Spanish clothes are built for relatively narrow frames. Check that zips and other fittings work properly. Women's clothes sizes translate as UK 8/USA 4/Spain 36, through to UK 18/USA 14/Spain 46. Men's clothes in Spain are usually in small (waist 28–30), medium (waist 32–34), large (waist 36–38) and extra-large (waist 38–40).

5 Crafts and Souvenirs

The Costa Blanca offers plenty of choice for craft- and souvenir-hunting. Most towns have a particular speciality, and you can pick up delicious local wines, well-crafted blankets and woollen goods, the sticky treat *turrón*, or some pretty ceramics *(see pp74, 86)*.

6 Markets

Every town has a weekly market. These sell a wide array of local produce along with all kinds of cheap clothes, kitchen implements and, sometimes, crafts and souvenirs. Many of the larger towns and resorts have covered markets open daily (except Sundays), selling fabulous fresh produce. There are also regular craft markets on summer evenings along much of the coast. Tourist information offices have further details.

7 Haggling

Haggling is not practised in the bigger shops and stores, but you can enjoy bargaining for fresh produce or crafts at market stalls. Smaller shops will probably offer a discount if you wheedle convincingly enough.

8 Sales and Bargains

The annual sales (look for signs saying *Rebaixes* or *Rebajas*) are held in January and July/August. Most of the major department stores and some chain stores have a section devoted to *oportunidades*, where you can pick up some bargains if you're prepared to rummage.

9 Tax-free Shopping

Non-EU citizens are entitled to claim back value-added tax (*IVA* in Spanish) on goods and services costing over €90. Look for signs in shop windows indicating that they participate in the "Global Refund" scheme. Make sure you get a stamped receipt which shows the *IVA* component, and claim back the tax when you leave. *www.globalrefund.com*

10 Hypermarkets and Shopping Malls

The shopping mall phenomenon has hit Spain in a big way. Every large city and resort will have a shopping mall with supermarkets and all kinds of shops under one roof somewhere on the outskirts of town.

Left **City-centre *pensión*** Right **The balcony of a typical *pensión***

Top 10 Accommodation Tips

1 Hotels

Hotels are awarded between one and five stars depending on the level of facilities. (Note that this classification system doesn't take into account charm or levels of service.) Tourist offices have comprehensive lists of local hotels.

2 Hostales and Pensiones

These are usually, but not always, at the budget end. They may lack the facilities that hotels offer, but they are often friendlier and very comfortable. Like hotels, they are classified using a star system (one or two stars).

3 Youth Hostels

There are relatively few youth hostels on the Costa Blanca. Many get booked up with school trips in summer. While they offer very cheap accommodation, they are rarely central and may be no cheaper than a budget *pensión* or *hostal* (particularly if you are travelling in a group). Private hostels are popular with young backpackers.

4 Villa Rentals

Numerous companies offer villa rentals, ranging from simple apartments to quasi-palaces. The Internet and the travel pages of weekend newspapers are good sources of ads and information. It's also worth checking out the small ads on the online version of the *Costa Blanca News*, a local English-language newspaper. ✆ *www.costablanca-news.com*

5 Paradors

Paradors (*paradores*) are state-run hotels. They tend to be fairly dear, but they have good facilities and are often set in historic buildings. There are two on the Costa Blanca, both purpose-built; one in Xàbia (Jávea), the other in Puerto Lumbreras. Look out for special deals on the website, especially out of season. ✆ *www.parador.es*

6 Casas Rurales

Casas rurales – country houses for rent or offering B&B – are a growing phenomenon. They are often located in small inland villages, and vary hugely in terms of facilities. There's a list on the official Costa Blanca website. Noratur has details of *casas rurales* in Murcia. ✆ *www.costablanca.org* • *www.noratur.com*

7 Camping and Caravanning

Camping and caravanning are enormously popular on the Costa Blanca. Sites are graded by a star system (one to three) according to the facilities offered. Many of the larger sites have every imaginable facility, while inland sites are often far less grand. If you want to camp in the Regional Parks of the Sierra de Espuña or Calblanque, contact the park information offices in advance *(see also p131)*.

8 Package Holidays

Package holidays offer great value for money, but you usually end up in the larger resorts, which means that peace and quiet can be in short supply.

9 Booking Services

Tourist offices have details of accommodation but don't provide a booking service, although staff are usually happy to help. The official websites also have accommodation lists *(see Directory, p112)*. Otherwise, consult the Spanish tourist office in your home country.

10 Booking Online

There are countless online booking services, many offering substantial discounts on standard prices. It is also worth checking out the websites of big Spanish chains such as Melia and NH-Hoteles for special deals. Almost all hotels can be booked on their own websites. It's wise to follow up online reservations with a phone call. ✆ *www.hotelconnect.co.uk*
- *www.hotelopia.co.uk*
- *www.booking.com*
- *www.solmelia.com*
- *www.nh-hoteles.com*

Left **Huerto del Cura** Right **Hostería de Mont Sant**

Top 10 Luxury Hotels

1 Meliá Villa Gadea Beach Hotel, Altea

This hotel overlooks the sea and is located in the charming village of Altea *(see p38)*. Facilities include three lagoon-style pools, tennis courts, children's club and thalasso-spa. Dine in any one of five restaurants. *Partida de Villa Gadea • Map G4 • 966 81 71 00 • www.solmelia.com • €€€€*

2 Hostería de Mont Sant, Xàtiva (Játiva)

A former monastery tucked below Xàtiva's castle is the idyllic setting for this romantic hotel with pool, gym, sauna and elegant restaurant *(see p79)*. *Subida al Castillo s/n • Map E1 • 962 27 50 81 • www.mont-sant.com • €€€–€€€€€*

3 Huerto del Cura, Elx (Elche)

This large hotel sits amid the famous palm groves of Elx. The rooms are in bungalows set in luxuriant gardens. The facilities include a swimming pool. *Porta de la Morera 14 • Map Q1 • 966 61 00 11 • www.hotelhuertodelcura.com • €€€*

4 Hotel Buena Vista, Denia (Dénia)

The rooms of this rosy 19th-century mansion set in beautiful gardens are in dark wood with terra-cotta tiles and sumptuous fabrics. Most offer expansive sea views. There's a gym, sauna, pool and paddle tennis court. The restaurant is among the best in the region. *Partida el Tossalet 82 • Map H2 • 965 78 79 95 • www.buenavistadenia.com • €€€€*

5 Meliá Boutique Palacio de Tudemir, Orihuela

Orihuela is a beautiful, historic town, and this hotel occupies a restored 18th-century palace, complete with beamed ceilings and cupola. The restaurant is top-notch. *C/Alfonso XIII 1 • Map P2 • 96 673 80 10 • www.hotelpalaciodetudemir.com • €€€*

6 El Rodat, Xàbia

This charming hotel offers comfortable rooms, suites and villas set in jasmine-scented gardens. There are two pools, one indoor, one out; the outdoor pool overlooks the peak of Montgó. *C/Murciana 9 • Map H3 • 966 47 07 10 • www.elrodat.com • €€€*

7 Hotel El Montiboli, La Vila Joiosa (Villajoyosa)

Perched on a rocky bluff overlooking a cove, the Montiboli has airy rooms with terraces, as well as suites and bungalows. There are three pools, a tennis court, a gym and sauna. The beach is a few steps away. Two restaurants serve fine Mediterranean cuisine. *Partida Montiboli s/n • Map F4 • 965 89 02 50 • www.montiboli.es • €€€–€€€€€*

8 Hespería Alicante Golf Spa, Alicante (Alacant)

This glossy development boasts its own 18-hole golf course (designed by Seve Ballesteros, no less) and a fabulous spa. Rooms are smart and modern, with large bathrooms. *Avda de las Naciones s/n, Playa de San Juan • Map E5 • 965 26 86 00 • www.hesperia-alicante.com • €€€€–€€€€€*

9 Hyatt Regency La Manga, nr Cartagena

In the heart of this premier golf resort, the Hyatt Regency is a favourite with sports stars and other celebrities. It is also well geared toward families. *Los Belones • Map P5 • 968 33 12 34 • www.lamanga.hyatt.com • €€€€€*

10 Hotel Amérigo, Alicante

The only five-star hotel in the centre of Alicante, the Amérigo is located in a Dominican convent, which has been tastefully renovated. Its rooftop terrace boasts a heated swimming pool and enjoys impressive views of the Castillo de Santa Bárbara and the Old Town. *C/ Rafael Altamira 7 • Map U3 • 965 14 65 70 • www.hospes.es • €€€–€€€€*

Palm Beach, Benidorm

Price Categories

For a standard, double room per night (with breakfast if included), taxes and extra charges.

€	under €50
€€	€50–€100
€€€	€100–€150
€€€€	€150–€200
€€€€€	over €200

TOP 10 Resort Hotels

1 Hotel Bali, Benidorm

A giant even by the standards of Benidorm's dizzying skyscrapers, the four-star Hotel Bali, at 186 m (610 ft), is the tallest hotel in Europe. It's worth choosing your room carefully, as not all of them have a balcony or terrace. *C/Luis Prendes s/n • Map G4 • 966 81 52 00 • www.granhotelbali.com • €€–€€€€*

2 Palm Beach, Benidorm

For Benidorm at its most flamboyant, try this enormous hotel packed with enjoyably kitsch details. All the usual facilities, plus a special children's play area. *C/ Viena 2 • Map G4 • 965 85 04 00 • www.palm-beach-hotel.com • €€*

3 Hotel Sidi San Juan, Alicante (Alacant)

Perfectly located on the Playa de San Juan, this sleek modern hotel has bright rooms, plenty of facilities, and two golf courses close by. Make sure you ask for one of the larger rooms. *La Doblada s/n, Playa de San Juan • Map E5 • 965 16 13 00 • www.hotelessidi.es • €€€–€€€€€*

4 Roca Esmeralda, (Calp) Calpe

This hotel sits right on the Levante beach, and offers bright, modern rooms. Choose from no fewer than four pools (one indoors and three out, including one for kids). *C/Ponent 1 (Playa de Levante) • Map G3 • 965 83 61 01 • www.rocaesmeralda.com • €€–€€€*

5 Meliá Altea Hills, Altea

This striking modern complex set on the edge of the pretty village of Altea, has five-star amenities – notably, enormous bathrooms and spectacular sea views. The hotel is surrounded by tropical gardens and boasts an outdoor pool, sports centre and spa. *C/Suecia s/n • Map G4 • 966 88 10 06 • www.solmelia.com • €€€–€€€€€*

6 Tano Resort, Gandía-Playa

A large, white-painted complex set around a pool, with plush rooms. Facilities include tennis court, football pitch, gym and outdoor pool. The only drawback is that it's about 1 km (half a mile) to the beach. *Partida de la Redonda s/n • Map F1 • 962 84 53 93 • www.tanoresort.es • €€*

7 Barceló Lodomar, San Pedro del Pinatar

A vast complex of rooms and apartments, with a gym, pools and a spa specializing in thalasso-therapy. The hotel sits on the edge of the San Pedro del Pinatar Regional Park, a paradise for bird-watchers. The Mar Menor beaches are about 500 m (547 yards) away. *Rio Bidasoa 1 • Map P4 • 968 18 68 02 • www.barcelo.com • €€–€€€*

8 La Sella Golf Resort and Spa

Overlooking the prestigious La Sella golf course in the foothills of the Montgó Natural Park, this is one of the most luxurious resorts in the whole region. The spa is one of the finest in Spain. *C/Alquería de Ferrando • Map H2 • 966 45 40 54 • www.lasellagolfresort.com • €€€–€€€€€*

9 Oliva Nova Golf, Oliva

A handsome seafront complex, the Oliva Nova is set around an 18-hole golf course designed by Seve Ballesteros. Most rooms and suites have sea views. Some even have private pools. *Urb. Oliva Nova Golf s/n • Map G2 • 902 38 37 36 • www.olivanovahotel.com • €€€–€€€€€*

10 Hotel del Alba, Mutxamel

A good base from which to discover the Costa Blanca, this hotel was opened in 2007. Facilities include a spa and sauna, outdoor and indoor pools, and beauty treatments. The hotel is surrounded by an 18-hole golf course. *C/Vespre 10 • Map E5 • 965 95 95 95 • www.hmc-hotels.com • €€–€€€*

Left **Huerto de la Virgen de las Nieves** Right **Posada del Mar**

Top 10 Stylish Hotels

1 Molí del Canyisset, La Font d'En Carròs

Converted from a 17th-century rice mill, this spectacular hotel (with pool) mixes traditional and ultra-modern styles. Some of the rooms are wheelchair-accessible. *Ctra La Font d'en Carrós s/n • Map F2 • 962 83 32 17 • www.hotelcanyisset.com • €€€*

2 Huerto de la Virgen de las Nieves, Xàtiva (Játiva)

This delightful, rosy-pink, 19th-century *finca* is surrounded by orchards and pine groves. Each of the nine rooms and suites is filled with antiques and paintings. The Huerto de la Virgen de las Nieves makes a good base for exploring beautiful Xàtiva, hiking in the sierras, or just relaxing by the pool. *Avda de la Murta 10 • Map E1 • 962 28 70 58 • www.huertodelavirgendelasnieves.com • €€–€€€*

3 Hotel Casa Lehmi, Tàrbena

This beautifully restored *finca* is set in mountains about 30 km (18 miles) from the coast. There are just eight spacious and very elegant rooms in an adjoining annexe. The excellent facilities include pool, tennis court and sauna. *Partida El Buscarro 1–3 • Map G3 • 965 88 40 18 • www.casalehmi.com • €€€€*

4 NH Rincón de Pepe, Murcia City

Easily the most stylish hotel in Murcia city, NH Rincón de Pepe exudes an air of old-fashioned formality. The celebrated cocktail bar "La Muralla" is built around the original Arabic wall. Its restaurant *(see p109)* is one of the best in the region. *C/ Apóstoles 34 • Map U6 • 968 21 22 39 • www.nh-hoteles.com • €€€–€€€€*

5 Casa del Maco, Benissa

This luxurious country hideaway in the foothills of the Lleus Valley has just four rooms, with beamed ceilings. There's a large terrace and pool. The romantic restaurant serves fine French cuisine with Mediterranean and Belgian influences. *Pou Roig s/n • Map G3 • 965 73 28 42 • www.casadelmaco.com • €€–€€€*

6 Hotel L'Estació, Bocairent

An eccentric former railway station, with one room adapted for disabled guests. Nice touches include aromatherapy kits and fruit baskets in each room. Well located for the nearby Sierra Mariola. *Parc de l'Estació • Map D3 • 962 35 00 00 • www.hotelestacio.com • €€–€€€*

7 Finca El Almendral, Relleu

Each of the rooms in this beguiling hotel is named after one of the deadly sins, and is decorated accordingly. Stroll through almond groves, hike in the mountains, or be sinfully slothful by the pool. *Partida El Terme • Map F4 • 965 94 13 83 • www.elalmendral.es • €€€*

8 La Casa Vieja, Rugat

Beautiful rooms, attentive service and thoughtful details make La Casa Vieja the perfect country retreat. There's a huge fireplace to huddle round in winter, an excellent restaurant, and a pool. *C/Horno 4 • Map F2 • 962 81 40 13 • www.lacasavieja.com • €€–€€€*

9 Posada del Mar, Denia (Dénia)

A medieval mansion has been restored to house this stylish hotel, with 16 rooms and nine suites, some with spectacular terraces. Each room is individually decorated with an elegant mixture of old and new. *Plaza Drassanes 2 • Map H2 • 966 43 29 66 • www.laposadadelmar.com • €€€–€€€€*

10 Pensión Oliva, Oliva

On the fringes of maze-like old Oliva, this pretty inn has five simple but stylish rooms. Two rooms are suitable for families, and one is wheelchair-accessible. There is also a lovely sun terrace *C/ San Luís 35 • Map G2 • 653 60 69 14 • www.pensionoliva.com • €*

Hotel Al Sur

Price Categories

For a standard, double room per night (with breakfast if included), taxes and extra charges.

€	under €50
€€	€50–€100
€€€	€100–€150
€€€€	€150–€200
€€€€€	over €200

Top 10 Seaside Charmers

1 Hotel Casa La Trancada, Isla Tabarca

Escape the hubbub of the resorts and appreciate the tranquil beauty of the Isla Tabarca *(see pp24–5)* at this 18th-century former fisherman's house. All four rooms are truly charming. There's also an excellent breakfast. *C/Motxo 12 • Map E6 • 630 50 35 00 • www.latrancada.com • €€–€€€*

2 Hotel Al Sur, Calabardina

A delightful hotel in a quiet village. Arches and terraces give the place a seductive Arabic feel. There is no restaurant or pool, but uncrowded beaches are just steps away, and there are plenty of local places to eat and drink. *C/Torre de Cope 24 • Map L6 • 968 41 94 66 • www.halsur.com • €€*

3 Hotel Rosa, Denia (Dénia)

Just 20 m (66 ft) from the beach, this modern hotel offers rooms and self-catering bungalows. There is a reasonably priced restaurant and big pool with toddlers' area. *Ctra de las Marinas, Km 1 • Map H2 • 965 78 15 73 • www.hotelrosadenia.com • €€*

4 Hotel Jávea, Xàbia (Jávea)

This classic seaside hotel just steps from the old port has friendly staff and spotless rooms – some have balconies overlooking the port and pebbly beach. *C/Pío X 5 • Map H3 • 965 79 54 61 • www.hotel-javea.com • €€*

5 Hostal Loreto, Denia

This congenial, family-run hotel tucked away in the picturesque old quarter of Denia is housed in a former convent dating back more than four centuries. The staff are charming. The rooms are modest but well equipped. Some have balconies overlooking the narrow street below. *C/Loreto 12 • Map H2 • 966 43 54 19 • www.hostal loreto.com • €–€€*

6 La Racona, Denia

Located on the fringes of the Montgó Natural Park, this family-run hotel has rooms and self-catering bungalows, most with views of the sea or the mountains. There's a small gym, a pool, tennis courts and a restaurant. *Camí Ample 19, Ctra Les Rotes • Map H2 • 965 78 79 60 • www.hotel-laracona.com • €€–€€€*

7 Hotel Gema, Teulada-Moraira

A simple hotel set in gardens, with swimming pool. Relaxed, friendly and ideal for families. There's a cheerful café-bar and restaurant (the latter open only in August). The beach is just 300 m (330 yards) away. *Cabo Estaca de Bares 11 • Map H3 • 965 74 71 88 • www.gemahotel.com • €€*

8 Villas La Manga, La Manga del Mar Menor

This charming development beside the Mar Menor offers 60 studios in whitewashed villas. There's a café in the summer months, plus pools for adults and children. The beaches of the Mar Menor are only 30 m (100 ft) away – those of the Mediterranean, just a little further in the other direction. *Gran Vía Km 3 • Map Q4 • 968 14 52 22 • www.villas lamanga.es • €€–€€€*

9 Parador de Jávea, Xàbia

This bland and boxy 1970s four-star parador has a stunning setting right on the beach, and it's surrounded by lush tropical gardens. The large, light rooms have terraces overlooking the Mediterranean. Facilities include pool, gym and sauna. There's a fine restaurant. *Avda del Mediterráneo 233 • Map H3 • 965 79 02 00 • www.parador.es • €€€–€€€€*

10 Balneario La Encarnación, Los Alcázares

Entering this winsome former spa hotel on the Mar Menor is like stepping back in time. The rooms are simple but charming, the service delightfully old-fashioned and courteous. Full-board only. *C/Condesa 8 • Map P4 • 968 57 50 07 • €€*

Hotel Termas

Top 10 Mountain Retreats

1 Hotel La Façana, Biar

This rural hotel offers nine charming rooms (two of them are triples) right in the centre of Biar; all of them have views of the church and the town hall. The excellent restaurant serves a range of local delicacies. ✆ *Plaza de la Constitución 2 • Map D4 • 965 81 03 73 • www.lafasana.com • €€*

2 Hospedería Molino del Río Argos, nr Caravaca de la Cruz

A 16th-century mill on the banks of the River Argos has been converted to house six apartments and a double room. There is a pool, a terrace with fountains, orchards, and endless rolling sierras right on the doorstep. ✆ *Camino Viejo de Archivel • Map K2 • 968 43 33 81 • www.molinodelrio.com • €€*

3 Hotel Els Frares, Quatretondeta

Get away from it all in this tiny mountain village of just 100 inhabitants. All-in walking holidays, plus a self-catering cottage. ✆ *Avda País Valenciano 20 • Map F3 • 965 51 12 34 • www.elsfrares.com • €€*

4 Pensión Castells, Castell de Castells

This utterly charming mountain inn is run by a friendly British couple. Delicious local cuisine is accompanied by wine straight from the barrel. Also on offer are tailor-made walking, biking and activity holidays. ✆ *C/San Vicente 18 • Map F3 • 965 51 82 54 • www.mountainholidays-spain.com • €€*

5 Hotel Termas, Archena

The oldest and grandest hotel in this palm-shaded spa village has rather characterless rooms, but its public areas are redolent of a glorious past. The hotel specializes in health and beauty packages, including massage, reflexology and thalassotherapy. ✆ *Balneario de Archena • Map M2 • 968 68 80 22 • www.balneariodearchena.com • €€–€€€*

6 Hotel Kazar, Ontinyent

This grand *palacete* (small palace) is nestled amongst lush gardens and palm trees in the centre of town. Its rooms are spacious and luxuriously appointed with attention to detail. ✆ *C/Dos de Mayo 117 • Map E2 • 962 38 24 43 • www.hotelkazar.com • €€€*

7 El Cortijo Villa Rosa, Caravaca de la Cruz

Just outside the village of Caravaca de la Cruz is this complex of four farmhouses. Each has been lovingly restored to offer rustic charm with modern comfort. There is a communal pool, BBQ area and lovely grounds. ✆ *Paraje Chuecos • Map K2 • 968 70 87 63 • www.cortijovillarosa.com • €€*

8 Hospedería Rural Molino de Felipe, Mula

One of the last working flour mills in Spain (dating back to the 16th century), this is also a wonderful hotel. There's walking in the nearby Sierra Espuña, a gym and a refreshing pool. ✆ *Paraje Ribera de los Molinos • Map L2 • 968 66 20 13 • www.paralelo40.org/molinofelipe • €*

9 Hotel Cenajo, Moratalla

In a region with limited accommodation options, this historic, primrose-yellow hotel is set about 30 km (18 miles) from the village, on the shores of a reservoir. Facilities include swimming pools, tennis courts and a gym. A good base for hiking, biking and riding in the surrounding sierras. ✆ *Embalse del Cenajo s/n • Map K1 • 968 72 10 11 • www.hotelcenajo.com • €€–€€€*

10 Mas de Pau, nr Penáguila

This handsome farmhouse set in the remote valley of Penáguila is surrounded by dramatic mountain scenery. Rooms are on the small side; the five wooden *cabañas* are a better bet. There's a bar and restaurant (both popular with locals), an indoor swimming pool, and a fitness area. ✆ *Ctra Alcoy-Penáguila Km 9 • Map F3 • 965 51 31 58 • €€*

Hotel El Paraíso

Price Categories

For a standard, double room per night (with breakfast if included), taxes and extra charges.		
	€	under €50
	€€	€50–€100
	€€€	€100–€150
	€€€€	€150–€200
	€€€€€	over €200

TOP 10 Budget Hotels

1 Hotel Los Ángeles, Benidorm

A friendly two-star hotel in the heart of Benidorm's old quarter, this is a better bet than the enormous, impersonal high-rise hotels. There's a simple café-bar, popular with locals, and the rooms are very good value. *C/Los Ángeles 3 • Map G4 • 966 80 74 33 • €€*

2 Zenit Murcia, Murcia City

Situated next to the Plaza de las Flores, this is one of the best bargains in the city. The rooms are well equipped, and the bathrooms are stuffed with lovely goodies. There's a good bar and a restaurant offering Mediterranean dishes, and staff are unfailingly helpful and courteous. *Plaza San Pedro 5–6 • Map T5 • 968 21 47 42 • www.zenithoteles.com • €€*

3 Los Habaneros, Cartagena

Sitting at the entrance to old Cartagena, this classic hotel is excellent value. The comfortable rooms are rather bland, but the restaurant is renowned throughout town. *C/ San Diego 60 • Map P5 • 968 50 52 50 • www.hotelhabaneros.com • €€*

4 Pensión Marina, Xàbia (Jávea)

This sweet, tiny *pensión* right on the seafront in the old port of Xàbia has been totally refurbished, and all rooms offer en-suite bathrooms. The location is perfect, and out of season, prices drop even further. *Avda de la Marina Española 8 • Map H3 • 965 79 31 39 • €€*

5 Hotel San Miguel, Altea

This whitewashed seaside hotel has a popular restaurant serving plain but delicious meals. A huge terrace offers wonderful views of the sea and the buzzy promenade below. *C/Mar 65 • Map G4 • 965 84 04 00 • €–€€*

6 Hotel El Paraíso, nr Cabo Cope

A modest hotel bedecked with window boxes, in one of the most delightful small resorts on the Costa Cálida. Rooms are basic but well-equipped, with air-conditioning, telephone and TV. There's a pleasant garden terrace, a restaurant and bar. *Ctra Cabo Cope–Calabardina • Map L6 • 968 41 94 44 • www.hotelelparaiso.net • €€*

7 Hostal Les Monges Palace, Alicante (Alacant)

Book early for this wonderfully quirky *pensión*, housed in a former convent in the heart of the old city. The corridors are lined with works of art (including a Dalí sketch), and some rooms boast jacuzzis or four-posters. *C/San Agustín 4 • Map U2 • 965 21 50 46 • www.lesmonges.net • €–€€*

8 Hotel Madrid, Águilas

This turn-of-the-20th-century hotel has seen better days, but the old-fashioned rooms still retain some charm. The bar, an unreconstructed 1960s classic, is fabulous. The delightful owners couldn't be friendlier. They host regular dinner dances and live music events. The restaurant serves tasty home cooking. *Plaza Robles Vives 4 • Map L6 • 968 41 11 09 • www.hotelmadridaguilas.com • €–€€*

9 Hostal San Juan, El Campello

This comfortable hotel overlooking the sea, and right next to a tram stop, is just 20-minutes away from Alicante. Enjoy long walks along San Juan beach or relax by the swimming pool. There's also a restaurant. *Avda da Jaime I 110 • Map E5 • 965 65 23 08 • €€*

10 Hotel Nou Hostalet, Cocentaina

Cocentaina is a large industrial town in the foothills of the Sierra Mariola, with a beautiful, faded medieval core. It's a good base for walking. This simple, comfortable hotel has a pleasant restaurant and offers first-class service. *Avda Xativa 4 • Map E3 • 965 59 27 03 • www.nouhostalet.com • €–€€*

Left **Estudios San Nicolás** Right **Las Lomas Village and Spa**

TOP 10 Self-Catering

1 Estudios San Nicolás, Alicante (Alacant)

An ingenious mix of hotel rooms and self-catering accommodation, Estudios San Nicolás is set in Alicante's seductive old quarter, overlooking the 17th-century Concatedral de San Nicolás. The four pristine studios have large en-suite bathrooms and small kitchen areas. ✆ *C/San José 5 • Map U2 • 965 14 01 12 • www.casasannicolas.com*

2 Casa La Calçada, Bocairent

This beautiful, old *casa rural* in the lovely medieval quarter of Bocairent features a well-equipped kitchen and dining room, plus bunk beds (sleeping eight). It is perfect for families and for those who wish to enjoy the peace and quiet of this medieval village and its surrounding areas. ✆ *Mossen Hilario 32 • Map D3 • 610 35 81 87 • www.bocairent-turistic.com*

3 Letting in Spain

This online company lets villas, apartments and bungalows around Torrevieja. Airport pickups are included in the price. Most properties are in the modern Ciudad Quesada resort, which is close to several golf courses, beaches and the Lagunas de la Mata and Torrevieja. ✆ *Avda de las Naciones 1–6, Ciudad Quesada-Rojales • Map Q3 • 965 72 54 10 • www.lettinginspain.com*

4 Casa Calixto III, Xàtiva (Játiva)

This *casa rural* is a handsome townhouse close to the cathedral in historic Xàtiva. Two double rooms and a quadruple make it perfect for families or larger groups. ✆ *Pza Calixto III 8 • Map E1 • 647 01 81 67*

5 Top Rural

You can search for rural houses, rural hotels, apartments, campsites and *cabañas* on this website, or narrow your search depending on the specific facilities you are interested in. ✆ *www.toprural.com*

6 Holiday Lets

This web-based company offers holiday lets in all areas of the Costa Blanca and Murcia region, covering both seaside and inland resorts. ✆ *www.holidaylets.net*

7 Las Lomas Village and Spa, Los Belones

For the ultimate in luxurious self-catering accommodation, look no further than Las Lomas, part of the prestigious La Manga resort. The 100 or so apartments are clustered round a golf course, and a fabulous spa offers the latest treatments. ✆ *Campo de Golf Los Belones, La Manga Club s/n • Map P5 • 968 33 12 34 • www.lamanga.laslomas.hyatt.com*

8 La Muralla, Cehegín

A pretty, whitewashed hotel at the very top of this magical village offers eight rooms and nine stylishly decorated self-catering apartments. The views across the ochre rooftops are breathtaking. The ideal location for exploring Cehegín's old quarter. ✆ *Plaza del Castillo s/n • Map K2 • 968 72 35 28 • www.hotel-lamuralla.com*

9 Casas Rurales, Caravaca de la Cruz

Set in gardens and orchards just outside the beautiful town of Caravaca de la Cruz, these well-equipped houses and apartments are grouped around a pool and barbecue area. Stylishly decorated, they sleep between two and 12 people. ✆ *Map K2 • 968 70 03 52 • www.solorural.com*

10 Owners Direct

This web-based company offers villas and apartments throughout the Costa Blanca, booked directly through the owners. Some places can be booked for as little as one night. The website also advertises B&B accommodation and guesthouses. ✆ *www.ownersdirect.co.uk*

Note: *Self-catering accommodation varies greatly in price according to size and quality. Check prices with individual owners.*

Left **Camping Xàtiva** Right **Sierra de Espuña: wooden *cabañas***

TOP 10 Camping and Caravanning

1 Sierra de Espuña

There are three very basic camping areas within the stunning Regional Park of the Sierra de Espuña; apart from four mountain refuges *(see p20)*, they are the only accommodation options within the park itself, and must be booked in advance from the park information office. Just outside the park, Camping Sierra Espuña has extensive facilities, including wooden *cabañas* for rent. *Ⓢ Map L3 • Visitor centre (Centro Ricardo Cordorníu) Parque Regional Sierra Espuña. 968 43 14 30. www.sierraespuna.com • Camping Sierra Espuña: El Berro. 968 66 80 38. www.campingsierraespuna.com*

2 Camping Bella Vista, Águilas

A big, friendly site 300 m (984 ft) from the beach, with shop, children's play area, table tennis, and a bar-restaurant close by. Wheelchair-accessible bungalows are also available. Open all year. *Ⓢ Ctra de la Vera Km 3 • Map L6 • 968 44 91 51 • www.campingbellavista.com*

3 Camping El Jardín, El Campello

Close to glorious San Juan beach, this site has all the usual amenities. There are few trees for shade, so get to the beach early in summer. Open all year. *Ⓢ C/Severo Ochoa 39 • Map E5 • 965 65 75 80 • www.campingeljardin.com*

4 Camping Xàtiva

This attractive site, just outside historic Xàtiva (Játiva), has a fantastic pool, lots of shady pitches and a laundry, but little else. It's an excellent base for mountain biking, hiking or sightseeing. *Ⓢ Ctra Genovés–Xàtiva • Map E1 • 962 27 14 62; 661 40 95 23 • www.vayacamping.net*

5 Caravanning-Camping Villasol, Benidorm

This enormous site, a few minutes' walk from the beach, is a virtual village. The facilities include two pools (one heated in winter), bars, a restaurant, satellite TV, supermarket, laundry and play areas. The site also rents out mobile homes. *Ⓢ Avda Bernat de Sarriá 13 • Map G4 • 965 85 04 22 • www.camping-villasol.com*

6 Camping La Marina, La Marina

This huge campsite in a seaside resort south of Santa Pola has every facility, from children's play areas, gym and large pool to hairdresser and on-site medical staff. *Ⓢ Ctra N-332 Km 76 • Map Q2 • 965 41 92 00 • www.campinglamarina.com*

7 La Puerta, Moratalla

This sleepy medieval village offers little visitor accommodation aside from this large campsite, set among trees close to the river. As well as tent and caravan pitches, it rents out cabins. Facilities include bar, restaurant, supermarket and laundry. *Ⓢ Ctra La Puerta • Map K1 • 968 73 00 08 • www.campinglapuerta.com*

8 Calblanque

The Regional Park of Calblanque *(see pp8–9)* incorporates one of the region's wildest stretches of coast and boasts stunning beaches. You can camp just outside the park at Caravaning La Manga. *Ⓢ Map P5 • Visitor information centre: La Jordana. 968 29 84 23 • Caravaning La Manga: Ctra Cartagena–La Manga, exit 11. 968 56 30 14. www.caravaning.es*

9 Camping Los Delfines, Playa Mojón

This huge site has big pitches on the beach near Puerto de Mazarrón resort. It also rents out wooden bungalows and is accessible for disabled travellers. *Ⓢ Ctra Isla Plana, Playa Mojón, Puerto de Mazarrón • Map M5 • 968 59 45 27 • www.campingsonline.com/delfines/*

10 Camping Mariola, nr Bocairent

Set amid mountains and almond groves, this pretty site has shady pitches and cabins for rent. Activities in the area include hiking, quad rental, and hot-air ballooning. *Ⓢ Ctra Bocairent-Alcoi • Map E3 • 962 13 51 60 • www.campingmariola.com*

***Note:** Campsites are always a budget option, though prices do vary according to the season. Contact individual sites for prices.*

General Index

Acknowledgements

The Author

Mary-Ann Gallagher is based in Barcelona, and has written and contributed to more than a dozen guidebooks on Spain.

Muchas gracias to Emma, Andy, Chris, Tony and Jesús at the Spanish tourist office in London, Victoria and Alfonso in Alicante, Guillermo, and all the kind staff at restaurants, hotels and tourist information offices across the Costa Blanca region.

Produced by DP Services, a division of Duncan Petersen Publishing Ltd, 31 Ceylon Road, London W14 0PY

Project Editor Chris Barstow
Designer Ian Midson
Picture Researcher Lily Sellar
Listings Researcher Guillermo Tascón
Indexer Hilary Bird
Proofreader Yoko Kawaguchi

Main Photographer Antony Souter
Additional Photography Marina Campello Herrero, John Miller and Susannah Sayler

Illustrator Chapel Design & Marketing

Maps James Macdonald (Mapping Ideas Ltd)

For Dorling Kindersley
Publishing Manager Kate Poole
Managing Editor Fay Franklin
Senior Cartographic Editor Casper Morris
DTP Jason Little
Production Rita Sinha
Design and Editorial Assistance Tessa Bindloss, Marina Campello Herrero, Nicola Erdpresser, Anna Freiberger, Katharina Hahn, Mary Ormandy, Marianne Petrou, Mani Ramaswamy, Sands Publishing Solutions, Word on Spain.

Picture Credits

Placement Key: t-top; tc-top centre; tl-top left; tr-top right; cla-centre left above; ca-centre above; cra-centre right above; cl-centre left; c-centre; cr-centre right; clb-centre left below; cb-centre below; crb-centre right below; bl-below left; bc-below centre; br-below right; b-bottom.

Every effort has been made to trace the copyright holders, and we apologise in advance for any unintentional omissions. We would be pleased to insert the appropriate acknowledgements in any subsequent edition of this publication. The publishers would like to thank the following individuals, companies and picture libraries for permission to reproduce their photographs:

AGENCIA VALENCIANA DE TURISMO: 13c; AISA-ARCHIVO ICONOGRÁFICO, S.A: *El Prendimiento*, 1763, by Francisco Salzillo; ALICANTE CITY TOURIST BOARD: 10-11c, 11tl, 12bl, 54tr; AQUOPOLIS, Torrevieja: 59tl. BRIDGEMAN ART LIBRARY: *The Fall of Granada in 1492*, 1890 by Carlos Luis Ribera y Fieve (1815-91), Burgos Cathedral, Burgos, Spain/Bridgeman Art Library, London 34tl. CAMPING SIERRA ESPUÑA: 131tr; CIRCULO INDUSTRIAL, Alcoi: 49tl; CORBIS: Jonathan Blair 13b; Jose Fuste Raga 117t; Reuters 45cr; COSTA BLANCA TOURISM BOARD: 10-11c, 11tl, 12bl. LA FINCA: 66tl. JARDÍN HUERTO DEL CURA: 7cr, 22bl, 22-23c. LA MANGA CLUB SA: 130tr; MUNDOMAR, Benidorm: 59b; MUNDOMARINO: www.mundomarino.es, 59t; MUSEO VILLENA: 73bl; MURCIA TURÍSTICA: 34b, 44tl, 44tr, 44cr, 45cl, 51cl. PALACETE RURAL LA SEDA: 66tr; PRISMA ARCHIVO FOTOGRÁFICO: 34tr, 35cr. LA RANA: 77tl; RENFE: 113tr; RESTAURANTE RINCON DE PEPE: 109tl; RESTAURANTE LA TANA: 99. TURESPAÑA: Krammer 31b; Pascual Lobo, J.J 50t.

For jacket credits see Contents page.

Phrase Book: Spanish

In an Emergency

Help!	**¡Socorro!**	soh-koh-roh
Stop!	**¡Pare!**	pah-reh
Call a doctor.	**¡Llame a un médico!**	yah-meh ah oon meh-de-koh
Call an ambulance.	**¡Llame a una ambulancia!**	yah-meh ah ahm-boo-lahn-thee-ah
Call the police	**¡Llame a la policía!**	yah-meh ah lah poh-lee-three-ah
Call the fire brigade.	**¡Llame a los bomberos!**	yah-meh ah lohs bohm-beh-rohs

Communication Essentials

Yes/No	**Sí/No**	see/noh
Please	**Por favor**	pohr fah-vorh
Thank you	**Gracias**	grah-thee-ahs
Excuse me	**Perdone**	pehr-doh-neh
Hello	**Hola**	oh-lah
Goodbye	**Adiós**	ah-dee-ohs
Good night	**Buenas noches**	bweh-nahs noh-chehs
What?	**¿Qué?**	keh?
When?	**¿Cuándo?**	kwan-doh?
Why?	**¿Por qué?**	pohr-keh?
Where?	**¿Dónde?**	dohn-deh?

Useful Phrases

How are you?	**Cómo está usted?**	koh-moh ehs-tah oos-tehd
Very well, thank you.	**Muy bien, gracias.**	mwee bee-ehn grah-thee-ahs
Pleased to meet you.	**Encantado/a de conocerle.**	ehn-kahn-tah-doh deh koh-noh-thehr-leh
That's fine.	**Está bien.**	ehs-tah bee-ehn
Where is/are …?	**¿Dónde está/están?**	dohn-deh ehs-tah/ehs-tahn
Which way to …?	**¿Por dónde se va a …?**	pohr dohn-deh seh bah ah
Do you speak English?	**¿Habla inglés?**	ah-blah een-glehs
I don't understand.	**No comprendo.**	noh kom-prehn-doh
I'm sorry.	**Lo siento.**	loh see-ehn-toh

Shopping

How much does this cost?	**¿Cuánto cuesta esto?**	kwahn-toh kwehs-tah ehs-toh
I would like …	**Me gustaría …**	meh goos-ta-ree-ah
Do you have …?	**¿Tienen …?**	tee-yeh-nehn
Do you take credit cards?	**¿Aceptan tarjetas de crédito?**	ah-thehp-than tahr-heh-tas-deh kreh-deee-toh
What time do you open/close?	**A qué hora abren/cierran?**	ah keh oh-rah ah-brehn/thee-ehr-rahn
this one/that one	**éste/ése**	ehs-teh/eh-seh
expensive	**caro**	kahr-oh
cheap	**barato**	bah-rah-toh
size (clothes)	**talla**	tah-yah
size (shoes)	**número**	noo-mehr-roh
white	**blanco**	blahn-koh
black	**negro**	neh-groh
red	**rojo**	roh-hoh
yellow	**amarillo**	ah-mah-ree-yoh
green	**verde**	behr-deh
blue	**azul**	ah-thool
bakery	**la panadería**	lah pah-nah-deh-ree-ah
bank	**el banco**	ehl bahn-koh
bookshop	**la librería**	lah lee-breh-ree-ah
cake shop	**la pastelería**	lah pahs-teh-leh-ree-ah
chemist	**la farmacia**	lah fahr-mah-thee-ah
grocer's	**la tienda de comestibles**	lah tee-yehn-dah deh koh-mehs-tee-blehs
hairdresser	**la peluquería**	lah peh-loo-keh-ree-ah
market	**el mercado**	ehl mehr-kah-doh
newsagent	**el kiosko de prensa**	ehn kee-ohs-koh deh prehn-sah
supermarket	**el supermercado**	ehl soo-pehr-mehr-kah-doh
travel agency	**la agencia de viajes**	lah ah-hehn-thee-ah deh bee-ah-hehs

Sightseeing

art gallery	**la galería de arte**	lah gah-leh-ree-ah deh ahr-teh
bus station	**la estación de autobuses**	lah ehs-tah-ee-ohn deh owtoh-boo-sehs
cathedral	**la catedral**	lah kah-teh-drahl
church	**la iglesia/la basílica**	lah ee-gleh-see-ah/lah bah-seel-i-kah
closed for holidays	**cerrado por vacaciones**	thehr-rah-doh porhr bah-kah-cee-oh-nehs
garden	**el jardín**	ehl hahr-deen
museum	**el museo**	ehl moo-seh-oh
railway station	**la estación de trenes**	lah ehs-tah-thee-ohn deh treh-nehs
tourist information	**la oficina de turismo**	lah oh-fee-thee-nah deh too-rees-moh

Staying in a Hotel

Do you have any vacant rooms?	**¿Tienen una habitación libre?**	tee-eh-nehn oo-nah ah-bee-tah thee-ohn lee-breh
double room	**Habitación doble**	ah-bee-tah-thee-ohn dob-bleh
with double bed	**con cama de matrimonio**	kohn kah-mah deh mah-tree-moh-nee-oh
twin room	**Habitación con dos camas**	ah-bee-tah-thee-ohn kohn dohs kah-mahs
single room	**Habitación individual**	ah-bee-tah-thee-ohn een-dee-vee-doo-ahl
room with a bath/shower	**Habitación con baño/ducha**	ah-bee-tah-thee-ohn kohn bah-nyoh/doo-chah
I have a reservation.	**Tengo una habitación reservada.**	tehn-goh oo-na ah-bee-tah-thee-ohn reh-sehr-bah-dah

Eating Out

Have you got a table for …?	**¿Tienen mesa para … ?**	Tee-eh-nehn meh-sah pah-rah
I'd like to reserve a table.	**Quiero reservar una mesa.**	kee-eh-roh reh-sehr-bahr oo-nah meh-sah
breakfast	**el desayuno**	ehl deh-sah-yoo-noh
lunch	**la comida/ el almuerzo**	lah koh-mee-dah/ehl ahl-mwehr-thoh
dinner	**la cena**	lah theh-nah
The bill, please.	**La cuenta, por favor.**	lah kwehn-tah pohr fah-vohr
waiter/waitress	**camarero/ camarera**	kah-mah-reh-roh/ kah-mah-reh-rah
fixed price menu	**menú del día**	meh-noo dehl dee-ah
dish of the day	**el plato del día**	ehl plah-toh dehl dee-ah
starters	**los entremeses**	lohs ehn-treh-meh-sehs
main course	**el primer plato**	ehl pree-mehr plah-toh
wine list	**la carta de vinos**	lah kahr-tah deh bee-nohs
glass	**un vaso**	oon bah-soh
bottle	**una botella**	oon-nah boh-teh-yah
knife	**un cuchillo**	oon koo-chee-yoh
fork	**un tenedor**	oon the-neh-dohr
spoon	**una cuchara**	oon-ah koo-chah-rah
coffee	**el café**	ehl kah-feh
rare	**poco hecho**	poh-koh eh-choh
medium	**medio hecho**	meh-dee-oh eh-choh
well done	**muy hecho**	mwee eh-choh

Menu Decoder

al horno	ahl ohr-noh	baked
asado	ah-sah-do	roast
el aceite	ah-thee-eh-teh	oil
aceitunas	ah-theh-toon-ah**s**	olives
el agua mineral	ah-gwa mee-neh-rahl	mineral water
sin gas/con gas	seen gas/kohn gas	still/sparkling
el ajo	ah-hoh	garlic
el arroz	ahr-rohth	rice
el azúcar	ah-thoo-kahr	sugar
la carne	kahr-ne	meat
la cebolla	theh-boh-yah	onion
la cerveza	thehr-beh-thah	beer
el cerdo	thehr-doh	pork
el chocolate	choh-koh-lah-the	chocolate
el chorizo	choh-ree-thoh	red sausage
el cordero	kohr-deh-roh	lamb
el fiambre	fee-ahm-breh	cold meat
frito	free-toh	fried
la fruta	froo-tah	fruit
los frutos secos	frooh-tohs seh-kohs	nuts
las gambas	gahm-bas	prawns
el helado	eh-lah-doh	ice-cream
el huevo	oo-eh-voh	egg
el jamón serrano	hah-mohn sehr-rah-noh	cured ham
el jerez	heh-rehz	sherry
la langosta	lahn-gohs-tah	lobster
la leche	leh-cheh	milk
el limón	lee-mohn	lemon
la limonada	lee-moh-nah-dah	lemonade
la mantequilla	mahn-teh-kee-yah	butter
la manzana	mahn-thah-nah	apple
los mariscos	mah-rees-kohs	shellfish
la menestra	meh-nehs-trah	vegetable stew
la naranja	nah-rahn-hah	orange
el pan	pahn	bread
el pastel	pahs-tehl	cake
las patatas	pah-tah-thas	potatoes
el pescado	pehs-kah-doh	fish
la pimienta	pee-mee-yehn-tah	pepper
el plátano	plah-tah-noh	banana
el pollo	poh-yoh	chicken
el postre	pohs-treh	dessert
el queso	keh-soh	cheese
la sal	sahl	salt
las salchichas	sahl-chee-chahs	sausages
la salsa	sahl-sa	sauce
seco	seh-koh	dry
el solomillo	soh-loh-mee-yoh	sirloin
la sopa	soh-pah	soup
la tarta	tahr-ta	tart
el té	teh	tea
la ternera	tehr-neh-rah	beef
las tostadas	tohs-tah-dahs	toast
el vinagre	bee-nah-gre	vinegar
el vino blanco	bee-noh blahn-koh	white wine
el vino rosado	bee-noh roh-sah-doh	rosé wine
el vino tinto	bee-noh teen-toh	red wine

Numbers

0	**cero**	theh-roh
1	**un**	oon-noh
2	**dos**	dohs
3	**tres**	trehs
4	**cuatro**	kwa-troh
5	**cinco**	theen-koh
6	**seis**	says
7	**siete**	see-eh-teh
8	**ocho**	oh-choh
9	**nueve**	nweh-veh
10	**diez**	dee-ehth
11	**once**	ohn-theh
12	**doce**	doh-theh
13	**trece**	treh-theh
14	**catorce**	kah-tohr-theh
15	**quince**	keen-theh
16	**dieciseis**	dee-eh-thee-seh-ess
17	**diecisiete**	dee-eh-thee-see-eh-teh
18	**dieciocho**	dee-eh-thee-oh-choh
19	**diecinueve**	dee-eh-thee-newh-veh
20	**veinte**	beh-een-teh
30	**treinta**	treh-een-tah
40	**cuarenta**	kwah-rehn-tah
50	**cincuenta**	theen-kwehn-tah
60	**sesenta**	seh-sehn-tah
70	**setenta**	seh-tehn-tah
80	**ochenta**	oh-chehn-tah
90	**noventa**	noh-vehn-tah
100	**cien**	theh-ehn
1000	**mil**	meel
1001	**mil uno**	meel oo-noh

Phrase Book: Valencian

In an Emergency

Help!	**¡Auxili!**	ow-gzee-lee
Stop!	**¡Pareu!**	pah-reh-oo
Call a doctor	**¡Telefoneu un metge!**	teh-leh-fon-eh oo oom meh-djuh
Call an ambulance.	**¡Telefoneu una ambulància!**	teh-leh-fon-eh-oo oo-nah ahm-boo-lahn-see-ah
Call the police.	**¡Telefoneu la policia!**	teh-leh-fon-eh-oo lah poh-lee-see-ah
Call the fire brigade.	**¡Telefoneu los bombers!**	teh-leh-fon-eh-lohs bohm-behrs

Communication Essentials

Yes/No	**Sí/No**	see/noh
Please	**Si us plau**	si us plau
Thank you	**Gràcies**	grah-see-uhs
Excuse me	**Perdoni**	puhr-thoh-nee
Hello	**Hola**	oh-lah
Goodbye	**Adéu**	ah-they-oo
Good night	**Bona nit**	bo-nah neet
Yesterday	**ahir**	ah-ee
Today	**avui**	un-voo-ee
Tomorrow	**demà**	duh-mah
What?	**¿Què?**	keh?
When?	**¿Quan?**	kwahn
Why?	**¿Per què?**	puhr keh
Where?	**¿On?**	ohn

Useful Phrases

How are you?	**¿Com està?**	kom uhs-tah
Very well, thank you.	**Molt bé, gràcies.**	mol beh grah-see-uhs
Pleased to meet you	**Molt de gust.**	mod duh goost
That's fine.	**Està bé.**	uhs-tah beh
Where is/are ...?	**¿On és/són ...?**	ohn ehs/sohn
Which way to ...?	**¿Per on es ...?**	puhr on uhs
Do you speak English?	**¿Parla anglès?**	par-luh an-glehs
I don't understand	**No l'entenc.**	noh luhn-teng
I'm sorry.	**Ho sento.**	oo sehn-too

Shopping

How much does this cost?	**¿Quant costa això?**	kwahn kost ehs-shoh
I would like ...	**M'agradería ...**	muh-grah-thuh-ree-ah
Do you have ...?	**¿Tenen ...?**	tehn-un
Do you take credit cards?	**¿Accepten targetes de crèdit?**	Ak-sehp-tuhn tahr-guh-tuhs duh kreh-deet
What time do you open/close?	**A quina hora obren/tancquen?**	Ah keen-uh oh-ruh oh- bruhn/ tan-kuhn
this one/that one	**aquest/aquell**	Ah-ket/Ah-kehl
expensive	**car**	kahr
cheap	**bé de preu/barat** bah-rat	be thuh preh-oo/
size (clothes)	**talla/mida**	tah-lyah/mee-thuh
size (shoes)	**número**	noo-mehr-oo
white	**blanc**	blang
black	**negre**	neh-gruh
red	**vermell**	vuhr-mel
yellow	**groc**	grok
green	**verd**	behrt
blue	**blau**	blah-oo
bakery	**el forn**	uhl forn
bank	**el banc**	uhl bang
bookshop	**la llibrería**	lah lyee-burh-ree-ah
cake shop	**la patisseria**	lah pahs-tee-suh-ree-uh
chemist	**la farmàcia**	lah fuhr-mah-see-ah
grocer's	**la botiga de queviures**	lah boo-tee-guh duh kee-vee-oo-ruhs
hairdresser's	**la perruqueria**	lah peh-roo-kuh-ree-uh
market	**el mercat**	uhl muhr-kat
newsagent	**el quiosc de premsa**	uhl kee-ohsk duh prem-suh
supermarket	**el supermercat**	uhl soo-puhr-muhr-kat
travel agency	**la agència de viatges**	la-jen-see-uh duh vee-ad-juhs

Sightseeing

art gallery	**la galería d'art**	lah gahl-luh-ree-yah dart
bus station	**l'estació de autobusos**	luhs-tah-see-oh dow-toh-boo-zoos
cathedral	**la catedral**	lah kuh-tuh-thrahl
church	**la església/ la basílica**	luhz-gleh-zee-uh/lah-buh-zee-lee-kuh
closed for holidays	**tancat per vacances**	tan-kat puhr bah-kan-suhs
garden	**el jardí**	uhl zhahr-dee
museum	**el museu**	uhl moo-seh-oo
railway station	**l'estació de tren**	luhs-tah-see-oh thuh tren
tourist information	**l'oficina de turisme**	loo-fee-see-nuh thuh too-reez-muh

Staying in a Hotel

Do you have any vacant rooms?	**¿Tenen una habitació lliure?**	teh-nuhn oo-nuh ah-bee-tuh-see oh lyuh-ruh
double room	**habitació doble**	ah-bee-tuh-see-oh doh-bluh
with double bed	**amb lit de matrimonio**	am lyeet duh mah-tree moh-nee
twin room	**habitació amb dos llits/amb llits individuals**	ah-bee-tuh-see-oh am dohs lyeets/am lyeets in-thee-vee-thoo-ahls
single room	**habitació individual**	ah-bee-tuh-see-in-thee-vee-thoo-ahl
room with a bath/shower	**habitació amb bany/dutxa**	ah-bee-tuh-see-see-oh am bahnyou/doo-chuh
I have a. reservation	**Tinc una habitació reservada.**	Ting oo-nuh ah-bee-tuh-see-oh reh-sehr-vah-thah

Eating Out

Have you got a table for …?	**¿Tenen taula per … ?**	teh-nuhn tow-luh puhr
I'd like to. reserve a table	**Voldria reservar una taula.**	Vool-dree-uh reh-sehr-vahr oo-nuh tow-luh
breakfast	**l'esmorzar**	les-moor-sah
lunch	**el dinar**	uhl dee-nah
dinner	**el sopar**	uhl soo-pah
The bill, please.	**El compte, si us plau.**	uhl kohm-tuh sees plah-oo
waiter/waitress	**cambrer/cambrera**	kam-breh/kam-breh-ruh
fixed price menu	**menú del día**	muh-noo thuhl dee-uh
dish of the day	**el plat del día**	uhl plat duhl dee-uh
starters	**els entrants**	uhlz ehn-tranz
main course	**el primer plat**	uhl pree-meh plat
wine list	**la carta de vins**	lah kahr-tuh thuh veens
glass	**un got**	oon got
bottle	**una ampolla**	oo-nuh am-pol-yuh
knife	**un ganivet**	oon gun-ee-veht
fork	**una forquilla**	oo-nuh foor-keel-yuh
spoon	**una cullera**	oo-nuh kool-yeh-ruh
coffee	**el café**	ehl kah-feh
rare	**poc fet**	pok fet
medium	**al punt**	ahl poon
well done	**molt fet**	mol fet

Menu Decoder

l'aigua mineral	lah-ee-gwuhl mee-nuh-rah	mineral water
sense gas/ amb gas	sen-zuh gas/ am gas	still/ sparkling
l'all	lahlyuh	garlic
al forn	ahl forn	roasted
l'arròs	lahr-roz	rice
les botifarres	lahs boo-tee-fah-rahs	cured meats
la carn	lah karn	meat
la ceba	lah seh-buh	onion
la cervesa	lah-sehr-ve-seh	beer
el filet	uhl fee-let	sirloin
el formatge	uhl for-mah-djuh	cheese
l'embotit	lum-boo-teet	cold meat
fregit	freh-zeet	fried
la fruita	lah froo-ee-tah	fruit
els fruits secs	uhlz froo-eets seks	nuts
les gambes	lahs gam-bus	prawns
el gelat	uhl djuh-lat	ice-cream
la llagosta	lah lyah-gos-tah	lobster
la llet	lah lyet	milk
la llimona	lah lyee-moh-nah	lemon
la llimonada	lah lyee-moh-nah-thuh	lemonade
la mantega	lah mahn-teh-gah	butter
el marisc	ulh mur-reesk	seafood
la menestra	lah muh-nehs-truh	vegetable stew
el pa	uhl pah	bread
el pastís	uhl pahs-tees	pie/cake
las patates	lahs pah-tah-tuhs	potatoes
el peix	pehs-kah-doh	fish
la pebre	pee-mee-yehn-tah	pepper
el pernil	uhl puhr-neel	cured ham
el plàtano	uhl plah-tun	banana
el pollastre	uhl puu-lyah-struh	chicken
la poma	lah poh-mah	apple
el porc	uhl pohr	pork
les postres	lahs pohs-truhs	desserts
rostit	rohs-teet	roast
la sal	lah sahl	salt
las salsitxas	lahs sahl-see-chuhs	sausages
la salsa	lah sahl-suh	sauce
sec	sehk	dry
el sucre	uhl soo-kruh	sugar
la taronja	lah tuh-rohn-djuh	orange
el te	uhl teh	tea
les torrades	lahs too-rah-thuhs	toast
la vedella	lah veh-theh-lyuh	beef
el vi blanc	uhl bee blang	white wine
el vi negre	uhl bee neh-greh	red wine
el vi rosat	uhl bee roo-zaht	rosé wine
el xai/el be	uhl shahee/uhl beh	lamb
la xocolata	lah shoo-koo-lah-tuh	chocolate

Numbers

0	**zero**	zeh-roh
1	**un/una**	oon/oon-uh
2	**dos/dues**	dohs/doo-uhs
3	**tres**	trehs
4	**quatro**	kwa-truh
5	**cinc**	seeng
6	**sis**	sees
7	**set**	set
8	**vuit**	voo-eet
9	**nou**	noh-oo
10	**deu**	deh-oo
11	**onze**	on-zuh
12	**dotze**	doh-dzuh
13	**tretze**	treh-dzuh
14	**catorze**	kah-tohr-dzuh
15	**quinze**	keen-zuh
16	**setze**	set-zuh
17	**disset**	dee-set
18	**divuit**	dee-voo-eet
19	**dinou**	dee-noh-oo
20	**vint**	been
21	**vint-i-un**	been-tee-oon
30	**trenta**	tren-tah
40	**quarenta**	kwuh-ran-tuh
50	**cinquanta**	seen-kwahn-tah
60	**seixanta**	seh-ee-shan-tah
70	**setanta**	seh-tan-tah
80	**viutanta**	voo-ee-tan-tah
90	**noranta**	noh-ran-tah
100	**cent**	sen
101	**cent un**	sen oon
1000	**mil**	meel
1001	**mil uno**	meel oo-noh

The following words crop up frequently in maps and on street signs. You may encounter them in their Spanish or Valencian forms, depending on which part of the Costa Blanca you are visiting.

English	Spanish	Valencian
Avenue	Avenida	Avinguda
Beach	Playa	Platja
Cape	Cabo	Cap
Castle	Castillo	Castell
Market	Mercado	Mercat
Museum	Museo	Museu
Square	Plaza	Plaça
Street	Calle	Carrer
Town Hall	Ayuntamiento	Ajuntament

Costa Blanca: Selected Index of Places